NEED to KNOW

AQA A-LEVEL POLITICS

Quick and easy revision

Key facts at your fingertips

ANDOVER COLLEGE

Rowena Hammal
Toby Cooper

HODDER EDUCATION
AN HACHETTE UK COMPANY

Hachette UK's policy is to use papers that are natural, renewable and recyclable products and made from wood grown in sustainable forests. The logging and manufacturing processes are expected to conform to the environmental regulations of the country of origin.

Orders: Please contact Hachette UK Distribution, Hely Hutchinson Centre, Milton Road, Didcot, Oxforshire, OX11 7HH. Telephone: +44 (0)1235 827827. Email education@hachette.co.uk. Lines are open from 9 a.m. to 5 p.m., Monday to Friday. You can also order through our website: www.hoddereducation.com

Lines are open from 9 a.m. to 5 p.m., Monday to Saturday, with a 24-hour message answering service. You can also order through our website: www.hoddereducation.co.uk.

ISBN: 978 1 5104 7714 8

First published in 2020 by
Hodder Education,
An Hachette UK Company
Carmelite House
50 Victoria Embankment
London EC4Y 0DZ

Impression number 10 9 8 7 6 5 4 3 2

Year 2024 2023

Typeset in India by Aptara

Printed and bound by CPI Group (UK) Ltd, Croydon, CR0 4YY

A catalogue record for this title is available from the British Library.

Contents

1 UK government 5

1.1 The British constitution 5

1.2 Parliament 9

1.3 The prime minister and Cabinet 16

1.4 The judiciary 24

1.5 Devolution 29

End of section 1 questions 32

2 UK politics 33

2.1 Democracy and participation 33

2.2 Elections and referendums 38

2.3 Political parties 49

2.4 Pressure groups 56

2.5 The European Union (EU) 59

End of section 2 questions 63

3 US politics 64

3.1 The US Constitution 64

3.2 Congress 69

3.3 The presidency 76

3.4 The judicial branch 82

3.5 The electoral process and direct democracy 87

3.6 US political parties 96

3.7 US pressure groups 99

3.8 Civil rights 102

End of section 3 questions 106

4 Political ideas 107

4.1 Liberalism 107

4.2 Conservatism 111

4.3 Socialism 115

End of section 4 questions 120

Getting the most from this book

This *Need to Know* guide is designed to help you throughout your course as a companion to your learning and a revision aid in the months or weeks leading up to the final exams.

The following features in each section will help you get the most from the book.

You need to know

Each topic begins with a list summarising what you 'need to know' in this topic for the exam.

Exam tips

Key knowledge you need to demonstrate in the exam, tips on exam technique, common misconceptions to avoid and important things to remember.

Key terms

Definitions of highlighted terms in the text to make sure you know the essential terminology for your subject.

Do you know?

Questions at the end of each topic to test you on some of its key points. Check your answers here: www.hoddereducation.co.uk/needtoknow/answers

Synoptic links

Reminders of how knowledge and skills from different topics in your A-level relate to one another.

End of section questions

Questions at the end of each main section of the book to test your knowledge of the specification area covered. Check your answers here: www.hoddereducation.co.uk/needtoknow/answers

1 UK government

1.1 The British constitution

You need to know
- what a constitution is
- the nature and sources of the UK constitution
- how the UK constitution has evolved
- two examples of constitutional changes since 1997
- what issues have arisen following recent constitutional changes
- the extent of rights in the UK

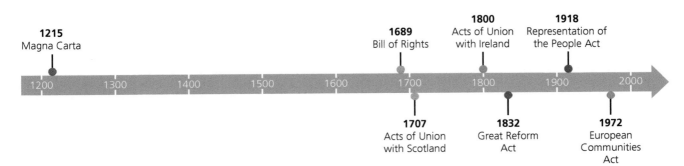

1215 Magna Carta

1689 Bill of Rights

1800 Acts of Union with Ireland

1918 Representation of the People Act

1707 Acts of Union with Scotland

1832 Great Reform Act

1972 European Communities Act

Figure 1 **Development of the UK constitution**

Functions of a constitution

In a liberal democracy, a constitution should:
- establish how a state/society is governed
- define the relationship between the state and the people
- show which bodies have which powers
- determine the relationship between different branches of government
- set out how different branches of government will work
- limit the power of government
- provide a defence for citizens from the government, through rights
- act as a higher form of law

> **Key term**
>
> **Constitution**
> A set of laws that determine the relationship, powers and responsibilities of the branches of government and people.

Nature of the UK constitution

Table 1 **Nature of the UK constitution**

Uncodified	▪ It is not in one single, authoritative document ▪ It is derived from many sources
Unentrenched	▪ The constitution is flexible and easy to change ▪ Constitutional laws have the same status as ordinary laws
Unitary	▪ Ultimate power is centralised in one place with laws applying equally to everyone ▪ Sovereignty is located in Parliament

Exam tip

It is worth comparing the UK constitution with other constitutions, like those of the USA and Germany, to comment on the advantages and disadvantages of the UK constitution.

The UK constitution rests on two key principles: parliamentary sovereignty and the rule of law.

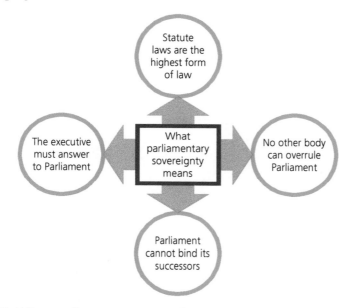

Figure 2 **What parliamentary sovereignty means**

Sources of the UK constitution

The UK constitution is made up of many different sources. Sometimes these conflict with each other and sometimes rules are forgotten or unclear.

Key terms

Uncodified Describes constitutional laws that are not set down in one single document.

Unentrenched Describes laws that are easy to change by a simple majority or new convention.

Unitary Where a nation is unified under one supreme government.

Parliamentary sovereignty Parliament is the supreme source of authority.

Rule of law The UK is governed by laws and legal processes.

Synoptic link

The unentrenched nature of the UK constitution makes constitutional reforms to Parliament, rights, elections and the Supreme Court easy to pass.

Table 2 **Sources of the UK constitution**

Statute laws	■ Laws passed by Parliament ■ They overrule any other laws
Conventions	■ Unwritten customs that acquire legal status ■ These can be altered by changing practices
Common law	■ Legal principles developed and applied by judges ■ Judicial review is used to establish the meaning of other laws
Authoritative opinion	■ Works that explain the meaning and workings of the constitution ■ They are taken as legal precedents when interpreting the constitution
Royal prerogative	■ Some of the traditional powers of the monarch can be exercised by the prime minister ■ Does not require the approval of Parliament ■ Prime minister can negotiate treaties, act as commander-in-chief of armed forces and use the power of patronage
Treaties	■ Agreements with foreign nations that impact on the workings of the UK ■ Treaties are negotiated by the government but subject to parliamentary approval

Changing the constitution is as simple as adding a new source or altering one of the existing sources.

Historic documents that have developed rights in the UK

Table 3 **Historic documents that have developed rights in the UK**

Magna Carta (1215)	■ Established the principle that the rule of law applied to everyone, including the king
Bill of Rights (1689)	■ Established the principle of parliamentary sovereignty
Act of Settlement (1701)	■ Prevented Catholics from marrying the monarch, ensuring that the monarchy would remain Protestant, as Parliament wished
Parliament Acts (1911 and 1949)	■ Prevented the House of Lords from blocking legislation passed by the Commons ■ 1911 Act allowed Lords to delay legislation for two years ■ 1949 Act reduced this to 1 year
European Communities Act (1972)	■ Gave EU law supremacy over UK law

Key terms

Statute law A law passed by Parliament; an Act of Parliament.

Convention A constitutional practice that is not written down.

Common law The process of judicial rulings which create legal precedents.

Authoritative opinion Expert writings that explain how the constitution operates in practice.

Treaties International agreements that impact on the way in which a country operates.

Exam tip

Make sure you know how each source of the constitution can be altered, with at least one example of each.

Constitutional changes since 1997

- New Labour's 1997 manifesto included a programme of constitutional reform. This included devolution of powers to new assemblies or parliaments in Scotland, Wales and Northern Ireland, with a range of new electoral systems.
- Some other Labour reforms are shown in Table 4.
- The Coalition government (2010–15) created the Fixed-term Parliament Act (2011), which removed the prime minister's power to call an early election without the consent of Parliament.
- The Leave victory in the 2016 EU referendum demanded the most significant constitutional reform of all.

Table 4 **Two examples of constitutional changes since 1997**

Reform	Detail	Impact
Lords reform, 1999	■ Removed all but 92 hereditary peers	■ Reduced the size of the Lords ■ Made the Lords more willing to challenge the Commons ■ Ensured no party had majority control in the Lords ■ Peers remained unelected — Labour's planned second phase of Lords reform is yet to happen ■ An attempt to create a mostly elected House of Lords failed to pass the House of Commons in 2012, and was abandoned by the Coalition government
The Human Rights Act, 1998	■ Codified the ECHR into statute law ■ Replaced much of common law ■ Turned negative rights into positive rights	■ Made it easier for people to defend their rights in the UK ■ Increased the power of the judiciary ■ Restricted Parliament's ability to pass laws ■ Led to conflict between Parliament and the judiciary

Key terms

Manifesto A set of policy proposals a party issues before an election.

Constitutional reform Any change to the workings of the UK constitution.

Peer A member of the House of Lords.

Synoptic links

- You will need to know about the 1997 election, so knowing New Labour's policies towards constitutional reform will help your understanding of the election.
- Constitutional reforms are often democratic reforms, so tie in with Paper 1.

Exam tip

You need to be able to analyse and evaluate two examples of constitutional changes since 1997.

Synoptic links

- The constitutional power of Parliament often causes conflict over rights with the judiciary and the role of the executive.
- The Miller case, 2017, confirmed that Parliament, not the prime minister, is responsible for triggering Article 50, and that referendums are only advisory.

Exam tip

You need to understand the issues and debates surrounding recent changes to the constitution.

Do citizens have extensive rights in the UK?

Table 5 **Do citizens have extensive rights in the UK?**

Yes	No
■ Britain signed the European Convention on Human Rights (ECHR) in 1951 and the Human Rights Act (1998) incorporated it into UK law ■ The 2010 Equality Act brought together many laws that prevented discrimination in areas including pay, sex, race, disability, religion and sexual orientation ■ Only an extremist government would remove citizens' rights, and removing rights would be very unpopular with voters	■ Rights are not entrenched as they can be easily removed by a simple majority of Parliament ■ When Britain leaves the European Union, citizens' rights will no longer be protected by EU law, which superseded UK law ■ Collective rights (e.g. a group's right to practice their religion) can threaten individual rights (e.g. the right not to be discriminated against because of sexuality or gender)

Key terms

Entrenched rights: Rights that are difficult to take away, e.g. in the US, citizens' rights can only be removed by amending the Constitution.

Collective rights The rights of a collective group of people.

Individual rights The rights of an individual person.

Do you know?

1 How has the UK constitution developed?
2 What is the nature of the UK constitution?
3 Why is Parliament sovereign?
4 What are the sources of the UK constitution?
5 How have historic documents contributed to the development of rights in the UK?
6 In what ways has the UK constitution been reformed since 1997?

Exam tip

You need to be able to analyse and evaluate areas where individual and collective rights agree, and areas where they are in conflict.

1.2 Parliament

You need to know
■ what Parliament is and how it is structured
■ the functions of Parliament
■ how Parliament scrutinises the executive
■ how legislation is passed
■ the Burkean, delegate and mandate theories of representation
■ the powers and significance of the Commons and Lords

Parliament is an assembly that meets to make and pass laws. In the UK, Parliament is bicameral, made up of:

- the House of Commons: the elected chamber in the UK Parliament.
- the House of Lords: the unelected chamber in the UK Parliament.

Features

Table 6 **Features of each chamber**

Commons	Lords
■ Elected by FPTP ■ Chaired by the speaker ■ Organised by party whips ■ The primary chamber ■ Enjoys parliamentary privilege ■ Regulates its own affairs	■ Unelected ■ Chaired by the Lord speaker ■ Composed of hereditary, life and spiritual peers ■ Limited by the Parliament Acts ■ Less controlled by whips ■ Not dominated by a single party

Functions

Table 7 **Functions of Parliament**

Legislate	■ Debate, discuss and amend Bills ■ Vote on Bills to become Acts of Parliament
Scrutinise	■ Scrutinise the work of government ■ Have an opposition tasked with holding the government to account
Debate	■ Debate major issues or government actions ■ Debates can be triggered by the public through the backbench Business Committee
Recruit ministers	■ Talented members of Parliament (MPs) are promoted to the government ranks ■ MPs learn the workings of Parliament before becoming ministers
Represent	■ Constituency interests ■ Party interests ■ The UK

Scrutiny of the executive

Table 8 **Ways in which Parliament can scrutinise the executive**

Questions to government ministers e.g. Prime Minister's Questions (PMQs)	■ Weekly questions to the prime minister or ministers allow MPs to publicly challenge the government ■ PMQs often appear to be unconstructive, and the atmosphere in the Commons can be aggressive ■ Television soundbites are frequently prioritised over genuine enquiry

Key terms

Bicameral Cameral meaning 'chamber' and 'bi' meaning two, refers to Parliament comprising two chambers.

Whips MPs who work for the party leader by telling party MPs what to do and how to vote.

Parliamentary privilege MPs cannot be prosecuted or sued for anything they say in the chamber of the House of Commons.

Member of Parliament (MP) Person who is elected to the House of Commons.

▶

Debate	■ Televised public debates allow members of both chambers to debate issues ■ MPs generally vote with their party, so it is not clear that debates have much influence
Select committees	■ Backbench MPs form committees on specific areas, e.g. Home Affairs and can call in ministers and other witnesses ■ Select committees publish reports that may criticise the government ■ Most select committee chairs are elected by MPs, so have authority from Parliament to challenge the government. Many are opposition MPs ■ The governing party has a majority on each committee and can ignore select committee reports
Amending and voting on legislation	■ All legislation can be amended by the Commons and the Lords and is voted on by both chambers ■ The government's party has a majority on public bill committees, so dramatic revision of a Bill is unlikely ■ Governments with a reasonable majority in the Commons will usually be able to pass their legislation, although minority government or those with a small majority may struggle
No confidence votes	■ Parliament can remove the prime minister with a no confidence vote ■ Rarely used as governments usually have a majority and MPs tend to be loyal

Key terms

Backbench MPs (or backbenchers) Ordinary MPs who do not hold a post in the government or the shadow government. They do not sit on the government or opposition front benches. They do the main work of Parliament, particularly in scrutiny and representation.

Public bill committee A small committee responsible for considering a Bill in detail and making amendments.

Bills Proposed laws introduced into Parliament for consideration.

Synoptic link

In September 2019, Boris Johnson withdrew the Conservative whip from 21 MPs who would not vote as his government wanted them to over Brexit.

Parliamentary debate and the legislative process

Parliamentary debates:
■ allow MPs to scrutinise the government
■ are mostly on topics chosen by the government
■ can be scheduled by the opposition parties on the 20 'opposition days' each year
■ generally happen in the second reading stage of the legislative process (see below)

Any Bill must go through five stages in each chamber before it can progress.

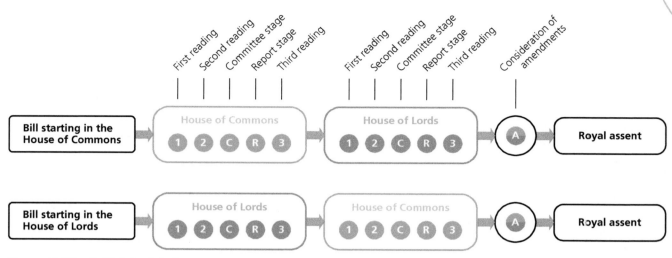

Figure 3 The British legislative process

- If a Bill is passed on all five stages, it repeats the process in the other chamber.
- Once passed by the second chamber, both chambers consider any proposed amendments.
- Once a final version of the Bill has been passed, it goes to the monarch to receive Royal assent.
- Royal assent turns the Bill into an Act of Parliament and makes it a law of the land.

Theories of representation

Table 9 Theories of representation

Burkean theory	■ MPs must vote in the best interests of their constituents ■ The role of an MP is that of a trustee ■ They have a duty to vote in line with their best judgement, even if their constituents disagree ■ Theory developed in the eighteenth century by Edmund Burke
Delegate theory	■ MPs have a duty to vote as their constituents wish ■ The role of an MP is that of a delegate ■ MPs might have to vote against their own best judgement, if a majority of their constituents disagree with them
Mandate theory	■ MPs have a mandate from their constituents to implement their party's manifesto pledges from the last election campaign ■ MPs must vote in support of their party so it can fulfil its manifesto commitments

Synoptic link

Following the 2016 EU referendum, MPs used different models of representation to justify their voting record during the Brexit process. Some Remainer MPs from Leave constituencies used Burkean theory to explain their refusal to vote for Theresa May's withdrawal agreement, for example.

Key terms

Royal assent The monarch's signature on a Bill, which turns it into an Act of Parliament.

Trustee A representative who votes in his/her constituents' best interests, regardless of his/her own views.

Delegate A representative who votes as his/her constituents wish him/her to, regardless of his/her own views.

Mandate Authority from the public for something to happen. A government that wins a majority has a mandate for the policies in its manifesto.

Campaign The period between the calling of an election, and the election itself, in which political parties attempt to persuade voters to support them.

Referendum A vote by the electorate on a single issue.

Role and influence of MPs and peers

Both MPs and peers:
- vote on legislation
- debate
- scrutinise government via committees
- may have a role in government or shadow government

MPs also:
- are democratically elected to represent their constituents
- deal with constituency casework and help constituents with redress of grievances
- select candidates for party leadership (in the Labour and Conservative parties) who the party membership then vote on
- ultimately decide which legislation is passed
- can remove the government with a vote of no confidence

Peers also:
- are unelected and do not represent constituencies
- provide an independent voice in Parliament — around 25% of Lords are crossbenchers
- provide specialist expertise from a broader range of professions and backgrounds than MPs
- play an important role in revising and amending legislation
- can ultimately be overruled by the Commons

Key terms

Redress of grievances MPs help their constituents to correct wrongs or 'grievances'. They might ask a question in Parliament on a constituent's behalf, or ask a government department to help.

Confidence motion A vote to determine whether the Commons still supports the government. If it loses, the government must resign.

The Salisbury Convention The Lords will not vote against a proposal from a winning manifesto.

The significance of the Commons and the Lords

The House of Commons is regarded as superior to the Lords due to its special powers of:
- financial privilege
- primacy over legislation
- the power to dismiss the executive

The superiority of the Commons over the Lords is upheld by the following laws and conventions:
- the Parliament Acts of 1911 and 1949
- the convention that the Lords cannot vote against any money Bills
- only the Commons may defeat the government on a confidence motion
- The Salisbury Convention prevents the Lords voting against a winning party's manifesto

- the 'reasonable time convention' prevents the Lords from delaying government business
- the Lords rarely block secondary legislation

Since the reform of the House of Lords in 1999, the Lords has become more effective at reviewing government legislation, checking the executive and representing public concerns. This is because:

- The reformed House of Lords has a large number of crossbenchers and no overall party in control.
- The reformed House of Lords has greater expertise on policy areas than a Commons comprised of career politicians.
- With no majority winner in 2010 and 2017, the Salisbury convention does not apply.
- Less unified parties mean Lords amendments are more likely to be supported by backbench MPs.

> ### Key terms
>
> **Secondary legislation**
> Legislation relating to how Acts are carried out and interpreted.
>
> **Select committees**
> Departmental committees that investigate and enquire into the workings of a government department.

Select committees

There is one select committee for each government department. Their purpose is to provide specialist scrutiny of the relevant department. They typically have 11 members, reflecting party make-up in the Commons.

> ### Exam tip
>
> If asked about the effectiveness of select committees, explain that they have been more independent since 2010 as their chairs are now chosen by secret ballot of the Commons, not by party whips.

Strengths and weaknesses of select committees

Table 10 **Strengths and weaknesses of select committees**

Strengths	Weaknesses
■ Detailed scrutiny of government policies and actions ■ Power to call witnesses and access government documents ■ Authority to recommend to the government ■ Increasing independence since 2010	■ Government majority on committees (usually) ■ Evasion of difficult questions ■ No power of enforcement ■ Members can use select committees to advance their own careers

Non-departmental select committees

Table 11 **Non-departmental select committees**

Backbench Business Committee	■ Decides on the topics to be debated during backbenchers' parliamentary time
Liaison Committee	■ Made up of the chairs of departmental select committees ■ Questions the prime minister twice a year

▶

| Public Accounts Committee | ■ Examines government expenditure
■ Ensures the taxpayer gets value for money |
| Public Administration and Constitutional Affairs Committee | ■ Examines constitutional reform
■ Examines the role of the civil service |

Lords select committees

Lords select committees:

- choose subjects to investigate
- often focus on broader, long-term issues that Commons select committees may not have time to address
- invite evidence, call witnesses, write reports
- scrutinise the government

Public bill committees

Public bill committees:

- are temporary Commons committees of 30–40 members that debate and suggest amendments to Bills
- meet in the committee stage of the legislative process
- are composed of a majority of MPs from the governing party
- have members who are chosen by party whips

In the Lords, the whole House meets to consider proposed legislation, rather than forming a public bill committee.

The role of the opposition

The largest party not in the government forms the official opposition, which:

- forms a government in waiting
- has right of first response to the government
- scrutinises specific departments
- receives an opposition fund to help challenge the government

The extent of Parliament's influence on government decisions

Factors affecting the relationship between Parliament and government include:

- the size of the government's majority
- the unity of the governing party/parties

Exam tip

Parliamentary power relates to the power of the government; things that make Parliament more powerful make the executive weaker and vice versa.

Key term

Opposition Those MPs who do not support or form part of the government.

Synoptic link

There is a fusion of powers between Parliament and the executive, so the topics need to be studied together.

- the popularity of the PM
- the nature of issues faced
- the strength of the opposition

Parliament's power over the government decreases with:
- a larger government majority
- a unified governing party
- a popular prime minister
- uncontroversial issues
- a weak or divided opposition

The government can attempt to limit the power of Parliament by:
- maintaining tight party discipline, allowing it to win Commons votes
- pressuring civil servants to be evasive in their answers to select committees (although civil servants have a duty to be helpful and accurate)
- choosing loyal MPs to fill the governing party's allocation of seats on select committees

Exam tip

You need to know how Parliament interacts with other branches of government. The fusion of the legislature and the executive means that government ministers are members of either the Commons or the Lords. Parliament also has the role of overseeing the actions of the executive. Parliament's laws are interpreted by the judiciary, which is separate from the other two branches of government.

Do you know?

1 What are the features of each chamber?
2 What are the functions of Parliament?
3 How is legislation is passed?
4 What are select committees, and how do they work?
5 What is the role of the opposition?
6 What are the factors that affect the relationship between the executive and Parliament?

Synoptic link

The UK Supreme Court can rule that Parliament's laws breach international agreements, e.g. the European Convention on Human Rights (ECHR), but Parliament remains sovereign and could withdraw from these.

1.3 The prime minister and Cabinet

You need to know

- what the executive is
- how policy is made
- the relationship between prime minister and Cabinet
- the difference between individual and collective responsibility
- the relationship between government and Parliament

The executive is the branch of government that makes things happen. It 'executes' the laws and decisions made in Parliament and runs the nation on a day-to-day basis.

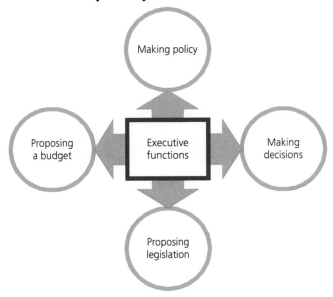

Figure 4 **Executive functions**

The whole government is vast, but the core executive consists of senior political figures and top civil servants.

The UK executive is made up of the following elements:
- the prime minister
- the prime minister's office
- the Cabinet
- the Cabinet Office
- junior ministers
- government departments
- the civil service

> ## Key terms
>
> Core executive The central group of advisors and ministers who work with the prime minister.
>
> Prime minister The leader of the executive branch.

The prime minister

To become prime minister a person must:
- be an MP
- be a party leader
- have the support of a majority of MPs to pass a budget
- be invited to form a government by the monarch

Functions of the prime minister

Table 12 **Functions of the prime minister**

Function	Description
Leadership	Shaping policy and acting as the spokesperson for the government
Running the government	Hiring and firing ministers, chairing Cabinet meetings and organising the civil service
Exercising the royal prerogative powers	Managing the armed services and making public appointments
Working with Parliament	Setting the agenda in the Queen's Speech and answering questions in Parliament
Representing the UK	Attending international summits and conferences as well as signing treaties

Powers of the prime minister

The prime minister has the power to:

- make treaties
- meet world leaders
- command the military
- run the civil service
- issue patronage and pardons
- control the legislative agenda
- make and amend delegated legislation

The Cabinet

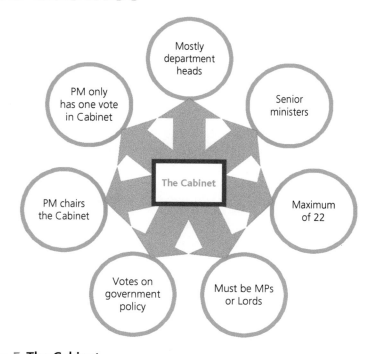

Figure 5 **The Cabinet**

PM only has one vote in Cabinet

Mostly department heads

Senior ministers

PM chairs the Cabinet

The Cabinet

Maximum of 22

Votes on government policy

Must be MPs or Lords

Functions of the Cabinet

Table 13 **Functions of Cabinet**

Function	Detail
Ratifying decisions	Decisions made elsewhere (bilateral meetings, Cabinet committees etc.) should be formally ratified by the full Cabinet
Decision making	Major issues can still be decided on by a formal discussion and vote in a full Cabinet meeting
Settling disputes	Disputes between senior ministers or government departments can be resolved during a meeting of the full Cabinet
Representing departments	Cabinet ministers are expected to champion the interests and needs of their departments
Advising the prime minister	Cabinet receives reports on parliamentary business, economic affairs, home and foreign issues. Based on these reports, Cabinet ministers can seek clarification and give advice to the prime minister

The Cabinet system

Table 14 **The Cabinet system**

Cabinet meetings	■ Usually once a week ■ Fixed seating and structure ■ Votes on issues where the prime minister is only one vote among all those cast and can therefore be defeated
Inner cabinet	■ Smaller group of the most important ministers who meet separately to the Cabinet ■ Decisions may be made by inner cabinet before being discussed by the whole Cabinet ■ Meetings may be more informal, e.g. Tony Blair's 'sofa government' ■ The Coalition's 'Quad' committee consisted of Conservatives David Cameron and George Osborne, and Liberal Democrats Nick Clegg and Danny Alexander, and acted as an inner cabinet from 2010–15
Cabinet committees	■ Sub-committees appointed by the prime minister for specific issues ■ Smaller and more focused than full Cabinet meetings ■ Prime minister decides membership of each committee ■ Collective responsibility of the whole Cabinet applies to decisions made by Cabinet committees
The Cabinet Office	■ A civil service department that organises the Cabinet ■ Cabinet secretariat carries out the key administration

Key terms

Inner cabinet A small group of the most senior ministers who meet separately to the main Cabinet.

Cabinet committee A group of ministers that takes responsibility for a specific aspect of government, e.g. the National Security Committee.

Collective responsibility All ministers must publicly support the decision of the government.

How policy is made

The UK has a Cabinet system and the Cabinet is the ultimate decision-making body:

- The prime minister sets the overall policies of the government.
- Department heads have expertise relevant to specific policies.
- Ministers receive advice from senior civil servants and special advisors.
- The prime minister sets the agenda for Cabinet meetings.
- Cabinet is free to discuss and debate issues.
- The prime minister decides when votes take place.
- Cabinet can vote to defeat the prime minister.
- Many decisions are also made in bilateral meetings and Cabinet committees.
- Cabinet is bound by collective responsibility once a decision has been made.

Civil servants are responsible for implementing policies once they have been decided, under the supervision of government ministers.

> **Synoptic link**
>
> UK Cabinet meetings are usually weekly, whereas the US Cabinet may only meet every few months. This reflects the greater political importance of the Cabinet in the UK.

The relationship between prime minister and Cabinet

- All prime ministers have the same core powers.
- Relationships between the prime minister and the Cabinet vary greatly depending on circumstances.

Table 15 Factors influencing the relationship between prime minister and Cabinet

Factor	Detail
PM free to appoint, promote or dismiss as he/she sees fit	The PM can appoint allies who will support his/her cause, e.g. David Cameron made his close ally George Osborne Chancellor of the Exchequer
Appointing rivals	The PM may appoint political rivals to the Cabinet to ensure their support, e.g. Boris Johnson was given the role of Foreign Secretary in Theresa May's Cabinet, until he resigned in July 2018
Developing rivalries	Rivalries within Cabinet may develop over time, e.g. Tony Blair initially had a strong partnership with his chancellor, Gordon Brown, but over time the Cabinet became divided between Blairites and Brownites
Party division	Cabinet may be divided between members of the party who agree with the PM and those who do not, e.g. the divisions between Brexiteers and Remainers in May's Cabinet

> **Synoptic link**
>
> In the UK's system of Cabinet government, the prime minister is 'first among equals'. In the USA, the president is the sole executive power, so his Cabinet officers are advisors who do not have collective responsibility.

Coalition	The PM has to take greater care to ensure the support of Cabinet during periods of coalition, as the other party's support is not guaranteed, e.g. David Cameron had to ensure that Liberal Democrat ministers in his Cabinet agreed with his policies
The power of the PM	Prime ministers who enjoy a large majority and strong party support can dominate their Cabinet, e.g. Tony Blair, Margaret Thatcher. Such PMs may be accused of presidentialism Weak leaders who lack a majority or significant party support struggle to control their Cabinet, e.g. Theresa May
Primus inter pares	The PM is 'first among equals' The PM can be outvoted by his/her Cabinet or even forced out of office, e.g. Margaret Thatcher after she finally lost the support of her Cabinet in 1990
Challenging events	Contentious events can create divisions within Cabinet, e.g. two Cabinet ministers resigned from Blair's Cabinet in protest against the 2003 invasion of Iraq

The difference between individual and collective responsibility

Collective responsibility

Collective responsibility means that:

- Cabinet discussion and disagreements are kept secret.
- Decisions made by the Cabinet are binding on all ministers; anyone not accepting must resign.
- If the government is removed by a confidence vote, all ministers must resign.

Examples of collective responsibility:

- **Iain Duncan Smith** resigned as work and pensions secretary in David Cameron's Cabinet in 2016 on the basis that he could not support the government's cuts to disability benefits.
- **Andrea Leadsom** resigned as leader of the House of Commons in Theresa May's Cabinet in May 2019 because she could not support the government's Bill for leaving the European Union, arguing that a hard Brexit would be better for Britain.

The prime minister may relax the rules on collective ministerial responsibility in the following circumstances:

- during referendums
- during coalitions
- during a free vote on a major issue
- to retain a key minister in the government

Key terms

Presidentialism A style of leadership that focuses on behaving like a president, separate from Parliament, rather than as one among equals in the Cabinet or Parliament. Prime ministers can use the Downing Street machine, bilateral meetings and agenda setting to dominate the Cabinet system.

Primus inter pares A Latin term that means 'first among equals'. It is used to describe the prime minister's status in the Cabinet.

Collective responsibility All ministers must publicly support the decision of the government.

Exam tip

You should know that the power of the Cabinet changes over time and is the inverse of the prime minister's powers. Cabinet will be more powerful when:

- there is little or no government majority
- the governing party is divided
- the prime minister has a weak media presence
- there are major controversial issues

Individual responsibility

A minister must take individual responsibility for:

- mistakes made by his/her department
- failures of policy decisions and implementation
- personal misconduct (breaking the Ministerial Code of Conduct)

Examples of individual responsibility:

- **Sir Thomas Dugdale** resigned as Minister of Agriculture in 1954. High-profile mistakes had been made by civil servants in relation to a compulsory purchase of farmland and, although he personally had not made any errors, he resigned because he was accountable for the actions of civil servants in his department.
- **Gavin Williamson** was sacked as Defence Secretary in 2019. Theresa May believed that he was responsible for leaking information from a National Security Council meeting to a newspaper.

> ### Exam tip
>
> You need to know a specific example of a minister resigning because of individual responsibility, and an example of a resignation caused by collective responsibility.

Key terms

Individual responsibility Ministers are responsible for their personal conduct and the actions of their departments.

Ministerial Code of Conduct A list of rules by which ministers are expected to abide in terms of personal and financial behaviour.

Accountability Ministers should expect consequences (e.g. resignation or sacking) if they make mistakes.

Examples of the power to dictate events and make policy

The power of the prime minister and Cabinet to dictate events and determine policy making varies depending on circumstances.

Introduction of the poll tax (1990)

- The poll tax was a flat-rate local tax introduced by Margaret Thatcher's government.
- Nearly all adults would pay the same amount of poll tax.
- There were mass protests, violent riots, and many refused to pay.
- Thatcher failed to win the first round of a leadership challenge outright.
- She resigned because she could not count on the full support of her Cabinet or party.
- The poll tax was quickly ended.

Invasion of Iraq (2003)

- Following the 9/11 terror attacks, Tony Blair pledged to support US President George W. Bush in his 'war against terror'.
- Blair wanted to join the 2003 US-led invasion of Iraq, as he believed Iraq had weapons of mass destruction (WMDs).
- Two Cabinet ministers resigned over the issue: Robin Cook and Clare Short.
- More than a million people marched against the war.
- Parliament voted to support the invasion, but 25% of Labour MPs voted against, as did the Liberal Democrats.
- Reports of WMDs turned out to be based on weak intelligence.
- The war lasted much longer than expected, with a far greater cost in terms of lives and finance.
- Iraq spent years in a state of civil war, and the wider region was destabilised.
- Blair was subsequently re-elected, but his reputation never recovered.

> **Exam tip**
>
> Remember that a prime minister's power to influence events often depends on the size of their majority and their control of their Cabinet.

> **Exam tip**
>
> Make sure you can analyse and evaluate the role of both the prime minister and the Cabinet in the poll tax and Iraq War examples.

Relations between government and Parliament

Relations between government and Parliament are influenced by a range of factors.

Table 16 **Factors favouring government and Parliament**

Factors favouring the government	Factors favouring Parliament
- The party whip system means that a government with a large majority can usually pass its legislation with ease - The government controls the legislative programme in Parliament - Ministers seldom take responsibility for mistakes by their departments (despite the convention of individual ministerial responsibility)	- Governments which lack a majority find it very difficult to pass legislation - Ministers are personally questioned in the House of Commons - Parliament scrutinises government via select committees

The process of exiting the European Union produced a broken relationship between government and Parliament in 2019:

- The House of Commons rejected the government's draft deal with the EU on three occasions.
- The Speaker of the House of Commons, John Bercow, defended the rights of Parliament to make a final decision on the Brexit deal, and was criticised by the government for a lack of impartiality.
- The Commons voted to take control of parliamentary business and held votes on possible alternatives, but could not find a majority for any of them.

- Theresa May resigned as prime minister after failing to convince Parliament to accept her Brexit deal.
- Boris Johnson prorogued Parliament in September 2019, but this was ruled unlawful by the Supreme Court.
- Parliament passed a law to prevent Johnson from taking the UK out of the EU without a deal.

Do you know?

1 What is meant by the executive?
2 What are the powers of the prime minister?
3 What are the main steps in the formation of policy?
4 What factors determine the relationship between prime minister and Cabinet?
5 What is the difference between collective and individual ministerial responsibility?
6 Can you analyse two examples of how the prime minister and Cabinet dictated events and made policy?
7 What factors influence the relationship between government and Parliament?

1.4 The judiciary

You need to know

- the role of the Supreme Court
- how justices are appointed
- the difference between judicial independence and neutrality
- the powers of the Supreme Court
- how the Supreme Court influences the government and the legislature
- what *ultra vires* means
- what judicial review means

Key terms

Supreme Court The highest legal authority within the UK.

Constitutional Reform Act, 2005 The law that created the Supreme Court and Judicial Appointments Commission.

The role of the Supreme Court

The Supreme Court was created in 2009 as part of the Constitutional Reform Act, 2005. The aims were to:

- create a clear separation of powers between the judiciary and other branches of government
- create a more open and transparent appointment process

The new Supreme Court replaced the Law Lords, who had sat in the House of Lords.

The Supreme Court's main functions include:
- acting as a final court of appeal on criminal and civil cases from England, Wales and Northern Ireland
- acting as a final court of appeal for civil cases from Scotland
- clarifying the meaning of constitutional law

Supreme Court appointments

Who qualifies?

Nominees to the Supreme Court must be:
- holders of high judicial office for at least 2 years or
- qualified practitioners (barristers and certain types of solicitors) for at least 15 years

The process

Vacancy occurs
Five-member selection commission created
Commission nominates a candidate
The lord chancellor (justice secretary) accepts or rejects the nominee
The lord chancellor notifies the prime minister
Prime minister recommends the nominee to the monarch
Monarch confirms appointment by issuing letters patent

Figure 6 **How appointments are made to the Supreme Court**

Most senior judges are appointed by the Judicial Appointments Commission (JAC). However, Supreme Court justices are appointed by an ad hoc five-member commission, comprising:
- the president of the Supreme Court
- the deputy president of the Supreme Court
- one member of the JAC for England and Wales
- one member of the Judicial Appointments Board for Scotland
- one member of the JAC for Northern Ireland

Key terms

Separation of powers The judiciary is separate and independent from Parliament and the government.

The judiciary The judicial branch of the government comprising all judges in the UK.

Synoptic link

Democratically, some argue the Supreme Court should reflect the population of the UK, but in 2019 only three were women, all were white, and all but one were over 60 years old.

Key term

Judicial Appointments Commission (JAC) An independent body created to recommend judicial appointments to the prime minister.

Key principles
Judicial independence

Figure 7 How judicial independence is maintained

Challenges to judicial independence include:
- political controversies derived from the Human Rights Act (HRA) rulings
- the power to suspend UK laws incompatible with EU law
- the increased use of judicial review
- greater media focus and scrutiny of the judiciary in a political context
- public criticisms made by politicians

Judicial impartiality

Figure 8 How judicial impartiality is maintained

Challenges to judicial impartiality include:
- limited range of backgrounds
- increasing media profile and scrutiny
- increasing willingness to criticise the government
- the lack of legal precedent regarding Brexit
- judges' own personal prejudices

Power of the Supreme Court
Judicial review

The main powers of judges are to carry out judicial review and clarify points of law.

Judges can:
- declare ministerial actions or the actions of official bodies to be *ultra vires*
- declare primary laws incompatible with the HRA
- declare and suspend laws incompatible with European law until British withdrawal from the EU

The power of judicial review has increased due to:
- the importance of EU law in the UK
- the codification of the European Convention on Human Rights into UK law under the Human Rights Act, 1998
- increasing conflict between Westminster and devolved bodies over political authority

Complaints can be taken to two higher courts:
- the European Court of Human Rights (not EU)
- the European Courts of Justice (dealing with EU law, such as the Factortame case)

Synoptic link

Brexit will have an impact on UK law as, potentially, Parliament will need to move a great deal of EU law into UK law. The European Court of Justice will probably no longer act as a higher court of appeal.

Key terms

Judicial review The process of reviewing actions by political figures or institutions to decide whether they are legal.

Ultra vires A declaration that a public official or body has acted beyond his/her/its powers.

Factortame case A legal case of 1990 that established a precedent that statute laws that undermine EU law can be suspended.

Synoptic links

- Judicial review is limited because Parliament is sovereign and can therefore ignore or overrule judicial decisions.
- In the USA, the power of judicial review is much stronger as the constitution itself has sovereignty.

The impact of the Supreme Court

Table 17 **The impact of the Supreme Court on government, the legislature and policy process**

Impact on government	■ Can rule that actions of the executive are incompatible with the HRA ■ Government may ignore it, e.g. it continued to deny prisoners the vote after the Court ruled against it in 2005 ■ Government can use its control of Parliament (if it has a majority) to pass new legislation overruling the Court's decision ■ The Court can rule that government ministers are acting *ultra vires*
Impact on the legislature	■ Fully independent from Parliament since 2009 ■ Factortame allows it to suspend some statute laws if they do not comply with EU law ■ Can declare statute laws incompatible with the HRA ■ Parliament remains sovereign so could repeal or amend the HRA if it chose to do so ■ The Court's judicial review in the Miller case strengthened the power of Parliament
Impact on the policy process	■ Laws made to comply with the HRA ■ Laws made to comply with EU law (this may no longer be the case after Brexit)

Synoptic links

■ In September 2019, the Supreme Court ruled unanimously that Boris Johnson's decision to advise the Queen to prorogue Parliament was unlawful, because it had the effect of preventing Parliament from carrying out its functions during the Brexit process.

■ This judgement limited the power of the executive and emphasised the sovereignty of Parliament.

Key term

The Miller case Supreme Court decision of 2017 that determined Parliament, not the prime minister, had the right to trigger Article 50.

Do you know?

1 What is the role of the Supreme Court?

2 How are justices appointed?

3 What the difference is between judicial independence and judicial impartiality?

4 What are the powers of the Supreme Court?

5 How does the Supreme Court influence the government and the legislature?

6 Why are *ultra vires* and judicial review important?

1.5 Devolution

You need to know
- what devolution is
- the roles and powers of the devolved bodies in the UK
- why there is debate around devolution in England
- the impact of devolution on government of the UK

Aims of devolution

Devolution refers to the transfer of political power from the central to a subnational government. When devolution was introduced in 1998 it was intended to:
- enhance democracy with greater representation
- decentralise control from London
- modernise the UK political system
- reduce nationalism in Scotland and Wales
- establish peace in Northern Ireland

Synoptic link

Devolution is a key element of constitutional reform and has impacted on the workings of Parliament.

Exam tip

Devolution is only about the transfer of political power, not sovereignty. Sovereignty remains in Parliament as, legally, Parliament can recall powers.

Devolved bodies

Table 18 **Devolution in 2018 (powers from 1998 unless shown)**

	Key powers	Devolved policy areas	Size of body and electoral system	Impact
Scottish Parliament and Government	■ Income tax (2016) ■ Primary legislation ■ Administrative	■ Taxation ■ Health ■ Environment ■ Education ■ Law ■ Elections ■ Welfare ■ Abortion	■ 129 MSPs in the Scottish Parliament (AMS)	■ Rise of SNP ■ Scottish independence referendum ■ Divergent policies and programme from UK (tuition fees) ■ West Lothian question
Welsh Assembly and Government	■ Tax varying powers (2014) ■ Primary legislation (2011) ■ Administrative	■ Limited tax varying ■ Health ■ Environment ■ Education ■ Tourism ■ Elections	■ 60 Welsh Assembly members (AMS)	■ Growth in devolution ■ Growth in support for devolution ■ Variations from England (prescriptions)

	Key powers	Devolved policy areas	Size of body and electoral system	Impact
Northern Ireland Assembly and Executive	▪ Corporation tax ▪ Primary legislation ▪ Administrative	▪ Health services ▪ Some welfare ▪ Environment ▪ Education ▪ Law ▪ Police ▪ Election	▪ 108 Assembly members (STV)	▪ Peace ▪ Implementation of the Good Friday Agreement ▪ Power sharing, until 2017
English mayors	▪ Administrative	▪ Transport ▪ Education ▪ Housing ▪ Social services ▪ Planning ▪ Environmental	▪ London Assembly (2000) = 25 AMs (AMS) ▪ Directly elected mayors in England and Wales (11 established in 2002, 15 by 2019) ▪ Metro mayors (2017), directly elected, one per combined authority (SV), six in total	▪ Transfer of administrative responsibility from central government to local level ▪ Elections allow accountability

Key terms

Scottish Parliament and Government The devolved legislature and executive for Scotland.

Welsh Assembly and Government The devolved legislature and executive for Wales.

Northern Ireland Assembly and Executive The devolved legislature and executive for Northern Ireland.

Good Friday Agreement The deal that set up devolved government in Northern Ireland. This ended the violent conflict between nationalists and unionists known as 'the Troubles'.

Power sharing The Good Friday Agreement said that power had to be shared between the two largest parties in Northern Ireland (unionists and nationalists). Power sharing collapsed in January 2017 following a dispute between the Democratic Unionist Party (unionists) and Sinn Fein (nationalists) leaving Northern Ireland without a government.

The devolved nations (Scotland, Wales and Northern Ireland) have no powers in certain areas including:

▪ foreign policy
▪ Brexit negotiations
▪ defence and national security
▪ income tax (Northern Ireland only — Scotland and Wales both have the power to vary the rate of income tax from that set by the UK government)

Impact of devolution
Debate about English devolution

The development of devolution has created a constitutional issue with the West Lothian question.

Table 19 **Does England need further devolution?**

Yes	No
■ England lacks its own assembly ■ EVEL was designed to solve the West Lothian question ■ Devolved regional assemblies could provide local devolution ■ To counter a rising sense of English nationalism	■ An English parliament would dominate UK government because England is so much bigger than the devolved nations ■ EVEL has had a limited impact so far ■ A devolved regional assembly was rejected by the northeast in 2004 ■ Expense

Exam tip

You need to know how devolution currently works in England and understand both sides of the debate regarding further devolution in England.

Impact on the UK government

Changes resulting from devolution include:

■ reducing the power of the UK Parliament as many areas are dealt with by the devolved bodies

■ limiting parliamentary sovereignty as it would be difficult for Parliament to remove devolved powers

■ creating a quasi-federal state

Table 20 **Has devolution been beneficial for the UK?**

Yes	No
■ It has improved democracy by decentralising decision making ■ Local regions are able to prioritise local concerns ■ Peace has been brought to Northern Ireland ■ A sense of Britishness remains, shown in the no vote in the Scottish independence referendum	■ It leads to unequal representation and the West Lothian question ■ Policy divergence means there are different standards of provision across the UK ■ It has increased nationalism, threatening the Union ■ Lack of national coherence on a range of policy areas

Key terms

West Lothian question The issue of MPs from devolved areas voting in Westminster on issues that do not affect their own constituents.

EVEL English Votes for English Laws was an attempt to address the West Lothian question, passed in 2015. Laws that apply to England only have an extra stage in the legislative process, allowing English MPs to vote against the law before it returns to the whole House of Commons.

Parliamentary sovereignty The principle that Parliament is the supreme law-making body.

Federal A nation with a two-tier system with power divided between central government and regional governments.

Synoptic links

■ The West Lothian question relates to democracy and the nature of representation.

■ Devolution impacts on the power of Parliament and parliamentary sovereignty.

Do you know?

1 What is devolution?
2 What powers do devolved bodies have in the UK?
3 Why do some people think England needs further devolution?
4 What is the impact of devolution on the government of the UK?

End of section 1 questions

1 Why has the UK constitution been criticised?
2 How significant has constitutional reform been?
3 Should the UK constitution be codified?
4 How effective a check is Parliament on the government?
5 How representative is Parliament?
6 Why has the House of Lords been reformed?
7 Which chamber of Parliament is more powerful?
8 Why are some prime ministers more powerful than others?
9 How powerful is the Cabinet?
10 What is collective responsibility?
11 Why was the Supreme Court created?
12 Why is the Supreme Court controversial?
13 What impact will Brexit have on the judiciary?
14 What are the UK's devolved bodies?
15 How has devolution affected the UK?

2 UK politics

2.1 Democracy and participation

You need to know
- what democracy means
- the different types of democracy
- how suffrage has changed since 1832
- the groups that campaigned for the vote
- how people participate in politics
- how patterns of participation have changed

Nature of democracy

- Democracy is rule by the people.

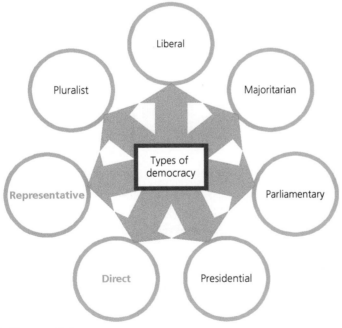

Figure 9 **Types of democracy**

Key terms

Direct democracy When decisions are made directly by the people.

Representative democracy When the people elect a representative to make decisions on their behalf.

Exam tip

Different types of democracy will result in different outcomes; this is not the same as being 'undemocratic'.

Direct and representative democracy

The UK is a representative democracy with some direct elements:
- Direct elements include referendums, petitions, citizens' juries and public consultations.
- Representative elements include elections, Parliament and devolved bodies.

Direct democracy

Table 21 **Advantages and disadvantages of direct democracy**

Advantages	Disadvantages
■ A purer form of democracy ■ Greater legitimacy to a decision ■ Improves political participation ■ Increases public engagement ■ Educates the public ■ It works	■ Not practical ■ Leads to tyranny of the majority ■ Undermines elected representatives ■ Can have low turnout ■ People do not understand the issues ■ People decide emotionally

Representative democracy

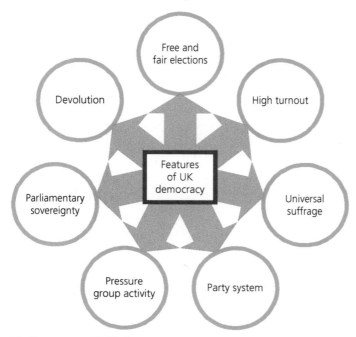

Figure 10 **Features of UK democracy**

Table 22 **Evaluation of representative democracy in the UK**

Element	Positive	Negative
Elections	Regular elections	The monarch and Lords are not elected
Turnout	Increasing since 2001 in general elections	Other elections usually below 50%
Universal suffrage	Everyone over 18 with few exceptions can vote	16- and 17-year olds and prisoners cannot vote
Party system	UK has a multi-party system	Safe seats and two-party dominance
Pressure groups	Campaign for and protect minority interests	Act in own self-interest rather than national good
Parliamentary sovereignty	Parliament has power to control the government	Parliament is usually dominated by the government
Devolution	Spreads power to local communities	Has created an imbalance in the UK system; the West Lothian question

---

Key term

Legitimacy The legal right to make decisions and take action.

Synoptic links

■ Referendums are the most common form of direct democracy; arguments about referendums apply to direct democracy.

■ In the USA, initiatives are used, which are like referendums but are initiated by the people, not the government.

Synoptic link

The result of the 2016 EU referendum created a constitutional crisis because it pitted direct democracy (52% voted Leave in the referendum) against representative democracy (the majority of MPs backed Remain). The sovereignty of Parliament meant that MPs were not obliged to carry out the referendum result.

How suffrage has changed since 1832

The franchise was extended many times between 1832 and 1969 as shown in Table 23.

Table 23 **The extension of the franchise**

Reform	Who could vote
Great Reform Act, 1832	Property owners/wealthy renters
Second Reform Act 1867	Doubled size of electorate by including working-class men in cities who were householders
Third Reform Act 1887	All men who were householders
Representation of the People Act, 1918	All men 21+ and women 30+ who were householders or married to a householder
Equal Franchise Act, 1928	All men and women 21+
Representation of the People Act, 1969	All men and women 18+

Chartists

The Chartists were a movement that:
- was active in the 1830s and 1840s
- campaigned to extend the franchise to all men over 21
- organised petitions signed by millions
- was dealt with harshly by the authorities, and ignored by Parliament
- became associated with violence
- had largely died out by 1850

The Second and Third Reform Acts later made progress towards some of the Chartists' demands.

Suffragists and suffragettes

From 1866 a campaign grew to give women the right to vote, dominated by two groups, the suffragists and the suffragettes.

Table 24 **Comparison of suffragettes and suffragists**

Suffragists	Suffragettes
The National Union of Women's Suffrage Societies (NUWSS)	The Women's Social and Political Union (WSPU)
Established in 1897	Established in 1903
Led by Millicent Fawcett	Led by Emmeline Pankhurst and her daughters

▶

Suffragists	Suffragettes
Internally democratic, meaning decisions were made by the whole membership, not just the leaders	Internally undemocratic, meaning the leaders could impose decisions and actions on other members
Open to everyone, both men and women	Only open to women
Used peaceful methods	Used violent methods

Debates regarding universal suffrage

Groups currently barred from voting:

- under 18s
- prisoners
- those sectioned under the Mental Health Act
- lords and monarch

Table 25 **Debates regarding universal suffrage**

Gender	■ Women traditionally seen as physically and mentally weaker and too emotional to vote ■ Claims that a woman's place was at home
Class	■ Elite worried that working class could not be trusted with vote ■ Seen as ill-informed and likely to vote socialist
Ethnicity	■ All ethnicities have equal voting rights
Age	■ 'Votes at 16' campaign aims to give 16- and 17-year-olds the vote ■ Some argue that under-18s do not have sufficient education or maturity to vote

Synoptic link

Lowering the voting age to 16 is supported by the Labour Party, Green Party, SNP and Liberal Democrats, and has happened in the Scottish Parliament and Welsh Assembly, and the 2014 Scottish independence referendum.

Exam tip

You need to be able to argue both sides of the 'votes at 16' debate effectively, even if you strongly support one side over the other.

Suffrage as a human right

- In 2005 the European Court of Human Rights ruled in *Hirst* vs *UK* that denying prisoners the vote was a breach of their human rights.
- This decision was supported by pressure groups such as the Howard League for Penal Reform.
- Many people believe that voting is a privilege that should not be entrusted to criminals.
- The UK government did not change the law, but in 2017 announced plans to allow a small number of prisoners to vote.
- In 2019, the Scottish government introduced legislation to give prisoners serving 12 months or less the right to vote.

Participation

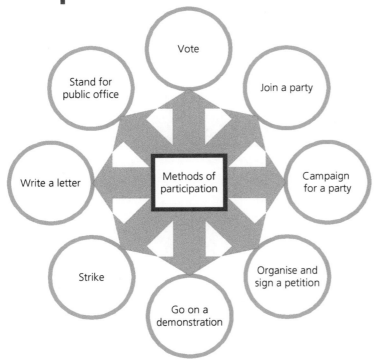

Figure 11 **Methods of participation**

Is there a participation crisis?

Table 26 **Is there a** participation crisis**?**

Yes	No
■ Falling turnout ■ Decline in party membership ■ Partisan dealignment may be a cause of low turnout ■ Decline of trade union membership and power	■ Increased turnout since 2001 ■ More parties ■ Labour membership has increased ■ Increased pressure group membership ■ Rise of social campaigns

Key terms

Participation crisis The concern that participation levels in politics are falling, undermining the legitimacy of British democracy.

Partisan dealignment People becoming less loyal to one core party.

Exam tip

A question on a participation crisis depends on perspective; in some ways there is and in other ways there is not a crisis, so stress this point in evaluating. Remember that the word 'crisis' suggests a critical situation that produces a significant and damaging impact.

Do you know?

1 What does democracy mean?
2 What is the difference between direct and representative democracy?
3 How has suffrage changed since 1832?
4 Which groups campaigned for the vote?
5 How do people participate in politics?
6 How have patterns of participation changed over time?

2.2 Elections and referendums

You need to know

■ the advantages and disadvantages of different types of electoral system
■ how the electoral system affects the party system
■ how patterns of voting behaviour have changed over time
■ three election case studies, including the 1997 election plus one before 1997 and one since
■ the use of referendums in the UK, and their impact

Elections play a vital role in democracies as they bestow democratic legitimacy on those elected to power as well as providing opportunities for representation and participation.

Key term

Democratic legitimacy
The consent of the people to be governed by the government, usually through elections.

Synoptic links

■ To be democratic, elections should be free and fair.

■ Rights of free speech and press help to make elections free, while the principle of one person one vote and equal-sized constituencies are designed to make elections fair.

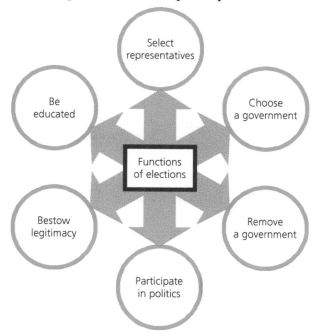

Figure 12 **Functions of elections**

Electoral systems

Table 27 Types of electoral systems

Type	Description	Example
Plurality	A candidate only needs one more vote than anyone else	First Past the Post (FPTP)
Majoritarian	Candidates are expected to achieve a majority of the votes (50%+1)	Supplementary Vote (SV)
Proportional representation	Votes are allocated on a proportional basis across large multi-member constituencies	Single Transferable Vote (STV)
Hybrid systems	Any system that combines a mixture of two other types of system	Additional Member System (AMS)

First past the post (FPTP)

The main voting system of the UK, FPTP, is a plurality system that requires only one more vote than anyone else to win a seat. Most issues of electoral reform concern the effects of FPTP on representation in Westminster.

Table 28 Workings of FPTP

Type	Plurality
Constituency size	Small, single member
Number of votes per person	One vote per person (as an X)
Voting for	A single candidate
Description	Within the constituency whoever has the most votes becomes the single representative for the whole constituency
Where used	UK general elections, most local council elections in England

FPTP tends to:

- benefit large parties with concentrated support
- lead to safe seats
- result in a few key marginal seats
- promote a two-party political system
- benefit smaller parties with concentrated geographical support
- result in single-party government
- disadvantage smaller parties with widespread support
- result in a winner's bonus where parties win many seats by small margins

> ### Exam tip
>
> You need to know the debates around the different types of electoral systems and be able to evaluate the strengths and weaknesses of each one.

> ### Key terms
>
> **Plurality** A vote in which a candidate only needs one more vote than other candidates to win.
>
> **Safe seat** Seat that remains loyal to one party and is unlikely to switch allegiance.
>
> **Marginal seat** Seat that can be won narrowly, with more than one party having a chance to win it.

Table 29 **Advantages and disadvantages of FPTP**

Advantages of FPTP	Disadvantages of FPTP
■ Simple ■ Traditional ■ Clear constituency result ■ Strong and stable government ■ Government accountability ■ Clear MP–constituency link ■ Excludes extremist fringe parties	■ Little choice ■ Minority representatives ■ Votes are of unequal value ■ Elective dictatorship ■ Does not always lead to single-party majority (2010 and 2017) ■ Unrepresentative governments ■ Disproportional outcomes ■ Excludes smaller parties

> **Exam tip**
>
> If analysing the problems with FPTP, be sure to support your argument with examples, e.g. UKIP's 3.9 million votes won just one Commons seat in 2015.

Supplementary vote (SV)

Table 30 **The workings of SV**

Type	Majoritarian
Constituency size	Small, single member
Number of votes per person	Two votes on a preferential basis (first choice and second choice)
Voting for	A single candidate
Description	If a candidate gains 50%+1 of the first-choice votes, he/she is elected. If not, all but the top two candidates are eliminated and the second-choice votes are redistributed to the top two candidates (if they were the second choice)
Where used	London and other elected mayors in England and the PCCs

Table 31 **Advantages and disadvantages of SV**

Advantages of SV	Disadvantages of SV
■ It makes it more likely that a candidate has majority support ■ It provides voters with more choice as they have two votes ■ Voters can show support for smaller parties and still choose a likely winner ■ To win, a candidate would require broad support ■ It would retain a strong MP–constituency link	■ Winning candidate is not guaranteed to get 50% of the total votes cast ■ It makes it possible for the second-placed candidate to win ■ It does not benefit smaller parties in a practical sense ■ There will still be many wasted votes ■ It is likely to promote more of a two-party system and be less representative than FPTP

Single transferable vote (STV)

Table 32 **The workings of STV**

Type	Proportional
Constituency size	Large multi-member (6–8)
Number of votes per person	As many votes as there are candidates
Voting for	Individual candidates on a preferential basis
Description	A formula is used to determine the quota of votes for one seat. Once a candidate reaches the quota, they are elected. The candidate with the fewest votes is eliminated and votes reallocated preferentially until the quota is reached and so on until all seats are filled
Where used	Northern Irish Parliament and Scottish local council

STV is the most proportional electoral system used in the UK. It is used in Northern Ireland as a means of ensuring widespread party representation as part of the Good Friday Agreement in 1998.

Table 33 **Advantages and disadvantages of STV**

Advantages of STV	Disadvantages of STV
■ Outcomes are proportional ■ STV helps to ensure votes have equal value ■ The final result is likely to be a government backed by 50% of the electorate ■ Voters have a wide degree of choice across parties and candidates ■ There will be very few wasted votes	■ The MP–constituency link is lost ■ It is complicated, leading to many spoiled ballots ■ It is likely to produce multi-party governments which may be unstable or have a weak mandate ■ The whole process means it takes a long time to get a result ■ People's fifth or sixth choice vote is not really considered a worthwhile vote

The additional member system (AMS)

Table 34 **The workings of AMS**

Type	Hybrid (FPTP and Closed Party List)
Constituency size	Small, single member and large regional constituencies
Number of votes per person	Two, one for a candidate under FPTP and one for a party under closed party list
Voting for	A single candidate and a party
Description	The candidate votes are counted and declared. Based on the results of the party list votes, party seats are 'topped up' from a list of candidates to ensure fairer representation
Where used	Scottish Parliament, Welsh Assembly, Greater London Assembly

> ## Key term
>
> BAME An acronym for 'black and minority ethnic', which covers all people of non-white or non-Anglo-Saxon/Celtic descent.

Table 35 **Advantages and disadvantages of AMS**

Advantages of AMS	Disadvantages of AMS
■ It retains the strong MP–constituency link for seats elected using FPTP ■ It allows for a more proportional representation ■ Voters have greater choice and can split their votes ■ The party list element allows some parties to increase the number of BAME and women candidates ■ It has eliminated the winner's bonus in the devolved areas ■ With enough support, single party government is possible ■ It allows voters to split their vote	■ It creates two categories of representatives who are held to account differently ■ With low levels of additional members, the proportionality is diminished ■ Most voters will vote the same way ■ Parties have control over who comes where on a party list ■ It has made it difficult for a strong and effective government to be formed ■ Usually a single party dominates the process

Table 36 **Comparison of electoral systems**

Function	FPTP	SV	STV	AMS
Strong stable government	Yes	Yes	No	Rarely
MP–constituency link	Yes	Yes	No	Mostly
Fairness of votes to seats	No	No	Yes	Mostly
Degree of choice	Limited	Moderate	Strong	Moderate
Party control	Limited	Limited	Limited	Moderate
Keeping out extremists	Yes	Yes	No	No
Easy for voters	Yes	Moderately	No	Moderately
Speed for result	Fast	Moderate	Slow	Moderate

> **Exam tip**
>
> For the UK paper, keep your answer focused on the electoral systems used in elections to the UK parliament and the devolved bodies, rather than those used in different countries.

Impact on the party system

- FPTP tends to produce a two-party system
- Majoritarian systems such as SV tend to produce a two-party system.
- Proportional systems such as STV usually result in a multi-party system, with coalition governments.

> **Exam tip**
>
> Be aware of the fact that the UK has had a coalition (2010–15) and minority government (from 2017). Voters have been increasingly supporting minor and regional parties. This has led to suggestions that the UK is now in effect a multi-party system and would benefit from a different electoral system.

> **Synoptic link**
>
> Party positions on electoral reform tend to be centred on how they do under FPTP; Conservatives and Labour tend to support it, other parties tend to demand reform.

Voting behaviour

Many factors influence how people vote:

Individual voting choices

People vote based on individual concerns, including:
- party policies
- major issues
- how the incumbent government has done in office
- the quality of the party leader
- the image of the party, local candidate and the party as a whole
- tactical voting

> **Key term**
>
> Tactical voting The process of using a vote to block a particular party because your preferred party is unlikely to win a seat.

In collating these concerns, voters will usually make a decision based on one of three theories:

- rational choice
- issue voting
- valence issues

Class

Until the 1970s, social class most often determined voting behaviour:

- middle-class voters were more likely to support the Conservatives
- working-class voters were more likely to support Labour.

Since the 1970s there has been class dealignment and partisan dealignment:

- Apart from 2017, the percentage of votes for the two main parties has declined, showing partisan dealignment.
- In 2017, the gap between the Conservatives and Labour was small in all classes, suggesting class has less impact on voting.
- Middle-class voters were more likely to vote to remain in the 2016 EU referendum than working-class voters of the same age.

Exam tip

Don't assume that class is the most important factor in determining voting behaviour. Class dealignment means that age and geography are now more important predictors of how people vote.

Age

Age voting suggests that parties will target policies to voters of a particular age bracket.

Key points:

- Before 1997, there was minimal party divide among the young.
- Since 1997, younger voters (below 35) tend to favour Labour far more.
- The older vote (55+) has nearly always gone Conservative, but the level of support has been increasing.
- Turnout among the young tends to be much lower than among older voters, which is why Labour has been less successful in elections than the Conservatives since 2010.
- In the 2016 EU referendum, a majority of 18–34 year olds voted to remain, while a majority of over-55s voted to leave.
- In 2017, age was the most important predictor of how people voted in the general election.

Key terms

Rational choice Voters weigh up their political options logically and vote for the party that will deliver the best result for them.

Issue voting Voters prioritise one issue above all others and cast their vote based on that issue.

Valence People vote based on the performance of the government in power.

Social class The socioeconomic group a person belongs to, which is based mainly on how they earn money.

Class dealignment People becoming less likely to vote as part of a social class.

Partisan dealignment People becoming less loyal to one core party.

Synoptic link

Election strategies will be determined by targeting key groups.

Exam tip

Make sure you know at least three examples of policies targeted at key age groups.

Geography

- Rural English areas and southern constituencies are more likely to be Conservative.
- Urban areas, particularly in London and the north, are more likely to be held by Labour, as is much of south Wales.
- Regional parties dominate in Scotland and Northern Ireland, and have an important presence in Wales.

Gender

Generally, men and women consider the same things important, such as taxation, and cast their vote in much the same way.

Areas where there are differences between men and women include war, nuclear power and weapons, and differences in core priorities, with men prioritising issues such as foreign affairs and military strength, while women tend to prioritise health and education policies.

Key points:
- Before 1997, women were more likely to vote Conservative.
- Since 1997, a higher proportion of women vote Labour.
- Men have tended to vote Conservative across the period.
- Since 1997 the difference between how men and women vote has become much less significant.
- Women were more likely to vote to remain in the EU than men.

Ethnicity

- BAME groups are significantly more likely to vote Labour than Conservative.
- White voters are more likely to vote Conservative than Labour.
- Turnout among BAME voters is typically lower (10–15%) than white voters.
- Within BAME voters there are differences, with black voters being much more pro-Labour than Asian voters.

Election case studies

Tables 37–39 show the context, results and impact on policy making of the 1979, 1997 and 2017 general elections.

Table 37 **The 1979 general election**

Political context	■ Followed 1978–79 'Winter of Discontent' strikes. ■ Labour leader James Callaghan faced new Conservative leader, Margaret Thatcher
Result	■ Conservative win ■ 43-seat majority ■ Middle class more likely to vote Conservative, working class more likely to vote Labour
Impact on policy making	■ Majority allowed Thatcher to privatise public industries, reduce strikes, and adopt radical new economic policies

Table 38 **The 1997 general election**

Political context	■ Conservatives in power since 1979 ■ Labour had new centrist leader, Tony Blair
Result	■ Labour landslide ■ 179-seat majority ■ Best result ever for Labour ■ Big Labour gains from middle and skilled working class
Impact on policy making	■ Huge majority allowed Blair to implement many policies, e.g. devolution, constitutional reform, national minimum wage, increased public spending

Table 39 **The 2017 general election**

Political context	■ Theresa May called a 'snap election', hoping for a mandate for her Brexit policies ■ Labour leader Jeremy Corbyn's poll ratings were very low ■ May assumed she would win a large majority
Result	■ Hung parliament ■ Conservative minority government dependent on a confidence and supply deal with the Democratic Unionist Party (DUP) ■ Conservatives lost 13 seats, Labour gained 30 ■ Seen as a 'return of two-party politics' ■ Conservatives' and Labour's combined share of the vote exceeded 80% for first time since 1980s (mainly due to collapse of UKIP vote)
Impact on policy making	■ May's leadership fundamentally weakened ■ Conservatives unable to deliver many manifesto commitments ■ May forced to negotiate Brexit while unable to control her divided MPs

Impact of the media

The way the media impacted on the general elections of 1979, 1997 and 2017 is shown in Figure 13 and Table 40.

Key term

Media Organisations that provide information to the public to inform, educate and entertain, covering newspapers, magazines, television, radio and the internet.

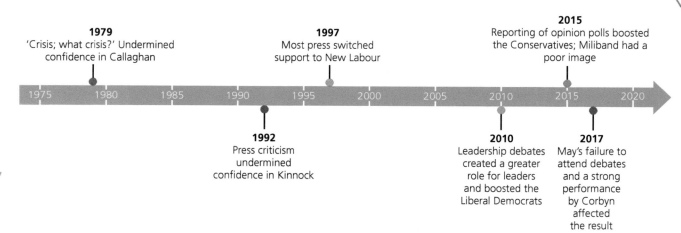

Figure 13 **The impact of the media on elections**

Table 40 **The impact of the media on the 1979, 1997 and 2017 general elections**

1979	■ New focus by media on leaders ■ Thatcher used television photo opportunities to raise her profile ■ The *Sun* switched support from Labour to Conservatives for the first time
1997	■ The *Sun* switched support from the Conservatives to Labour ■ Spin doctors managed Labour's interactions with the media to ensure that daily stories kept coverage 'on message'
2017	■ Jeremy Corbyn was widely criticised ■ Many newspapers, including the *Sun*, supported the Conservatives ■ Labour used social media to successfully reach out to younger people

Synoptic link

In the UK, political broadcasts are tightly regulated, but in the USA they are not.

Exam tip

Make sure you understand the role of the media, party policies, manifestos, campaigns and the party leader across three elections: 1997 and before, and one after.

Impact of party policies and manifestos

Party policies can be used to appeal to voters' self-interest, enthuse key groups of voters, inspire the party membership or to gain publicity.

■ Parties list their policies in their manifestos.

■ Manifestos are released at the start of election campaigns.

■ A good policy will help a party gain votes but a bad policy can cost it an election.

Table 41 **Key policies in the 1979, 1997 and 2017 general elections**

Election	Policy	Impact
1979	Conservative: ■ right to buy council houses ■ tax cuts to stimulate economy and cut unemployment	■ Motivated many council house residents to vote Conservative ■ Economic policies popular as unemployment was high

▶

Election	Policy	Impact
1997	Labour promised: ■ to cut class sizes ■ to cut NHS waiting lists ■ to reduce youth unemployment ■ not to raise taxes	■ Emphasised New Labour's centrist policies (known as the third way) and appealed to middle-class voters
2017	Conservative commitment to a hard Brexit	■ Won over many former UKIP voters
	Labour pledged to end tuition fees	■ Inspired a large number of young voters to vote and to vote Labour

Impact of leadership and campaigns

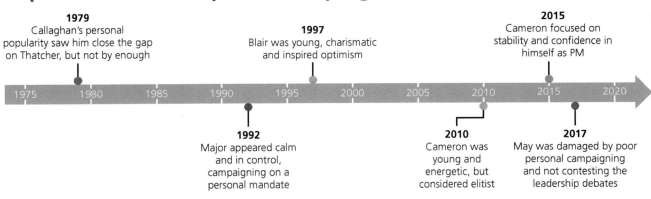

Figure 14 **Leaders in elections,1979–2017**

Table 42 **Leadership and campaigns in the case study elections**

Margaret Thatcher 1979	■ Effective 'Labour isn't working' campaign focused on high unemployment ■ Thatcher relatively unknown, some found her manner off-putting ■ Public interest and uncertainty surrounding a female prime minister
Tony Blair 1997	■ Negative campaigning from Conservatives: 'New Labour, New Danger' ■ Labour promised change: 'Because Britain deserves better' ■ Campaigns focused on party leaders ■ Blair was young (43) and inexperienced but charismatic
Theresa May 2017	■ May began with a huge lead in the polls, but was far less popular than Corbyn by election day ■ May refused to participate in television debates, and seemed aloof ■ Conservative campaign promised 'strong and stable' government but May's personality and policies were unpopular

Referendums

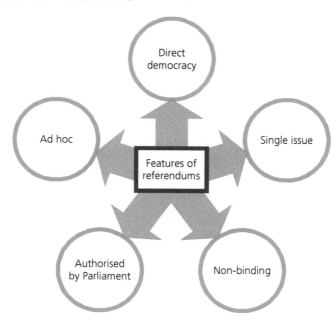

Figure 15 Features of referendums

Types of referendums

- Only three national referendums have been held (1975 EEC referendum, 2011 AV referendum, 2016 EU referendum), all on constitutional issues.
- Regional referendums have all dealt with devolution, e.g. the Scottish Independence referendum, 2014.
- Local referendums have tended to deal with policies rather than constitutional issues.

Why have referendums been called?

Referendums have been called over:

- constitutional change: Scotland, 1997; Wales, 1997; Wales, 2011; Scotland, 2014; EU, 2016
- Cabinet divisions: EEC, 1975
- party divisions: EU, 2016
- Coalition Agreement: AV, 2011
- testing public opinion: North East Assembly, 2004; Wales, 2011
- establishing peace: the Good Friday Agreement, 1998
- political pressure: Scotland, 2014; EU, 2016
- passing controversial local government decisions to voters: congestion charges and council tax increases

Synoptic link

As part of parliamentary sovereignty, permission to hold a referendum can only be granted by Parliament, which can ignore the decision. This was confirmed by the Miller case in 2017.

Synoptic link

There were growing calls for a second 'confirmatory' EU referendum in 2019 after Parliament refused to vote for Theresa May's EU withdrawal deal.

Synoptic link

The 2016 EU referendum result created a conflict between direct and representative democracy, and between popular and parliamentary sovereignty. 52% of the population voted to leave the EU, but the majority of MPs were Remainers. Britain could not leave the EU without Parliament's approval.

Referendums in a representative democracy

Table 43 Advantages and disadvantages of referendums in a representative democracy

Advantages	Disadvantages
■ They allow voters a direct say ■ They prevent the government pursuing unpopular policies ■ They give greater legitimacy to constitutional reforms ■ They enable more participation in politics ■ They achieve some exceptionally high levels of participation, e.g. 84.6% turnout, Scotland 2014 ■ They provide political education on core issues ■ They give some voters choices which were not offered by the parties running in their area	■ They over-simplify complex issues ■ They undermine Parliament ■ They allow politicians to pass difficult decisions to the public, promoting populist politics ■ They can be exploited by the government to its own advantage ■ They allow emotional, ill-informed decisions to be made ■ They can create public apathy if people do not understand or care about the issue, e.g. 42.0% turnout AV, 2011 ■ They allow unaccountable groups to manipulate the public

Do you know?

1 What are the advantages and disadvantages of each type of electoral system?
2 How does the electoral system affect the party system?
3 How have patterns of voting behaviour changed over time?
4 Why was the 1979 election significant?
5 Why was the 1997 election significant?
6 Why was the 2017 election significant?
7 What impact have referendums had in the UK?

Synoptic link

Referendums tend to promote pressure group activity as well as party activity, particularly as parties are often divided during a referendum.

2.3 Political parties

You need to know

■ how the Conservative, Labour, and Liberal Democrat parties have developed
■ how these three parties are structured
■ the debates around party funding
■ how the media interacts with parties
■ what factors influence the outcomes of elections
■ the impact of minor parties
■ how the UK is developing towards a multi-party system

Features of parties

Political parties:

- contest elections to win
- seek to gain power
- are internally democratic
- are regulated by the Electoral Commission

Functions and activities of parties

Parties play an important role in representative democracies.

Table 44 **Party functions and activities**

Functions	Activities
■ Representation of members ■ Participation in party activities ■ Education of the public ■ Recruitment of candidates for office ■ Policy formulation ■ Appointing party leaders ■ Forming a government ■ Scrutinising government	■ Canvassing ■ Delivering leaflets ■ Fundraising dinners ■ Selecting candidates ■ Local party meetings ■ 'Get out the vote' activities ■ Organising conferences

Classifying parties in the UK

Table 45 **UK** mainstream parties **and** minor parties

Mainstream	Minor parties

■ Conservatives
■ Labour
■ Liberal Democrats (created by combining the historic Liberal Party and the Social Democratic Party)
	■ Nationalists:
	  □ SNP
	  □ Plaid Cymru
	  □ English Democrats
	  □ Sinn Fein
	■ Unionists:
	  □ Democratic Unionist Party (DUP)
	■ Single issue:
	  □ Brexit Party
	  □ UKIP
	  □ Green Party
	  □ Christian Democratic Party
	  □ Independent Group for Change (founded 2019, aimed to become a mainstream party)

Key terms

Political parties Groups of people with similar beliefs, which promote ideas and/or causes that are important to their members.

Electoral Commission Oversees the running and organisation of referendums and elections.

Synoptic link

Parties play an important role in promoting democracy in the UK and can be contrasted with pressure groups.

Key terms

Mainstream parties Those parties that have been prominent for over 100 years and seek to represent the whole UK across many issues.

Minor parties Parties other than the three national parties. Includes single-issue parties, e.g. the Brexit Party, the Green Party, and nationalist parties, e.g. the SNP, Plaid Cymru.

Parties can also be classified by where they sit on the political spectrum between the left wing and right wing.

> ### Key terms
>
> **Political spectrum** A left–right spectrum that is based on a belief in the role of government and economic principles.
>
> **Left wing** Those who tend to favour greater government involvement and a regulated economy.
>
> **Right wing** Those who tend to believe in a smaller role for the government and a less regulated economy.

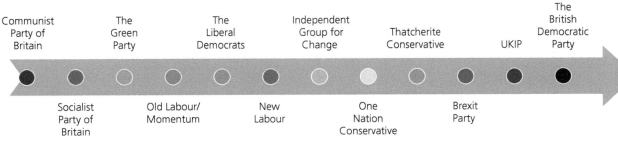

Figure 16 The British political spectrum

The mainstream parties

The Conservative party

The two main schools of thought in the Conservative Party are:

- **One nation:** Conservative ideology that society should provide support to ensure the gap between rich and poor is not substantial.
- **Thatcherite:** neo-liberal ideology that promotes the role of the individual and reduces the role of the state.

> ### Synoptic link
>
> Despite a party's name, it may not consistently follow an ideology; the Conservative party can be described as being liberal on economic matters.

Table 46 Key Conservative policies in 2017

Policy area	One nation	Thatcherite
Economy	■ Expand apprenticeships ■ Cap on energy prices	■ Raising the personal tax allowance ■ No rise in taxation, VAT or National Insurance ■ Private funding of social care
Home affairs	■ A law on 'victim's rights' ■ Commitments to protect EU residents already in the UK	■ Limit immigration ■ 'The snooper's charter' expanded the state's electronic surveillance powers
Health	■ Increase NHS spending	■ Integrate health and social care
Education	■ Increase grammar schools ■ Protect school funding per pupil	■ Continue supporting privately funded academies
Foreign affairs	■ Remain in the single market	■ Leave the EU

The Labour party

The two main schools of thought in the Labour party revolve around the ideas of:

- **Social democracy:** a form of socialism that operates within a capitalist system where the government promotes wealth redistribution to provide for greater social equality. Traditionally associated with Old Labour but more recently with Corbyn's Labour and the radical grassroots movement Momentum.
- **Third way:** a compromise between Old Labour social democracy and Thatcherite neo-liberalism; it is pragmatic and promotes individualism within a social framework. Adopted by Tony Blair's New Labour in 1994 and from 2010 promoted by the Labour pressure group 'Blue Labour'.

> ## Exam tip
> The Conservatives and Labour parties have both been deeply divided over Brexit — it is an issue that cuts across party lines.

Table 47 Key Labour policies from its 2017 manifesto show a mix of Old and New Labour ideas

Policy area	Old Labour	New Labour/Blue Labour
Economy	■ Increase minimum wage ■ Reintroduce a higher top rate of tax ■ Nationalisation of key industries, e.g. railways	■ Cut the deficit and balance the economy ■ No rise in VAT, National Insurance or income tax
Home affairs	■ Cap on non-EU workers ■ Restrict immigration ■ Scrap police crime commissioners	■ Establish a victim's law
Health	■ Additional funding for the NHS	■ Limit the profit private firms can make from the NHS
Education	■ Scrap university tuition fees ■ End charitable status of private schools	■ Create privately funded academies and expand them
Foreign affairs	■ Respect the referendum result and leave the EU (but by 2019 the party was divided on whether there should be a second referendum on Brexit)	■ Support a softer Brexit retaining the single market

The Liberal Democrats

The two main schools of thought in the Liberal Democrats are:

- **Classical liberalism:** a liberal ideology that promotes personal liberty and a limited role for the government in economic matters, associated with the Orange Book group.
- **Social liberalism:** a type of liberalism that focuses on individual rights and liberties for the individual that will ensure protection for all through government intervention to promote tolerance and equality.

> ## Exam tip
> You need to understand how the origins, ideas and development of the Conservative, Labour, and Liberal Democrats have helped shape their current policies.

Table 48 **Key Liberal Democrat policies in 2017**

Policy area	Orange Book	Social liberals
Economy	■ Deal with the deficit through a mixture of cuts and tax rises	■ Introduce a 1p tax increase to fund the NHS
Home affairs	■ New claimants to attend English language course before receiving Job Seeker's allowance	■ End imprisonment for drugs for personal use
Health	■ Integrate health and social care budgets	■ Increase NHS spending
Education	■ Maintain university tuition fees	■ A core curriculum including sex education
Foreign affairs	■ End nuclear deterrent ■ Remain in the single market	■ End nuclear deterrent ■ Remain in the EU

Party structures

Table 49 **Party structure of the Conservatives, Labour, and Liberal Democrats**

Conservatives	Labour	Liberal Democrats
■ Conservative Association in every constituency ■ Welsh and Scottish Conservative Party branches ■ National Conservative Convention makes decisions for the voluntary party ■ 1922 Committee of backbench Conservative MPs ■ Conservative Campaign Headquarters (CCHQ) ■ Governed by Board of the Conservative Party	■ Constituency Labour Party (CLP) in every constituency ■ Welsh and Scottish Labour branches ■ Governed by National Executive Committee (NEC) ■ MPs make up the Parliamentary Labour Party (PLP) ■ 14 trade unions affiliate to Labour, and many socialist groups	■ Federal structure (unlike two main parties) ■ Members belong to local, regional and national party ■ Governed by Federal Board ■ MPs make up the parliamentary party ■ Specified Associated Organisations (SAOs) have a particular focus

Party funding

To contest elections and fulfil their other functions, parties require funds:

■ Usually this comes from private sources, such as membership fees and wealthy donors or groups.

■ These sources have been declining since the 1970s.

■ Since then, the introduction of short money and Cranborne money has given some limited form of state party funding to opposition parties to help them hold the government to account.

Controversies in the late 1990s and early 2000s over where party money was coming from led to two new regulations:

■ Political Parties, Elections and Referendums Act, 2000

■ Political Parties and Elections Act, 2009

Plans to introduce full state funding are controversial and keenly debated as shown in Table 50.

Key terms

Short money State funds given to opposition parties in the House of Commons to cover costs and help fund scrutiny of the government.

Cranborne money State funds for opposition parties in the House of Lords.

State party funding Money given to political parties to cover their costs from the taxpayer.

Table 50 Arguments for and against the state funding of parties

For	Against
■ Reduce influence of wealthy individuals and groups ■ Improve the image of politics by making it appear less corrupt ■ Allow parties to compete on a more equal basis ■ Promote smaller parties outside Westminster ■ Reduce the need for politicians to waste time raising funds	■ Taxpayer money should not be spent funding party activities ■ Perception of corruption if taxpayer money is misspent ■ Parties will remain unequal depending on membership size and other factors ■ People may object to taxpayer money being given to fund extremist parties ■ Many fundraising activities involve democratic participation

Parties and the media

The relationship between parties and the media is important:

■ Party leaders regularly meet key media figures, e.g. Rupert Murdoch.
■ The *Daily Mail* and the *Telegraph* support the Conservatives.
■ The *Mirror*, and generally the *Guardian*, support Labour.
■ Other newspapers change their endorsement.
■ The BBC must remain politically neutral but is regularly criticised by parties for biased reporting.
■ Jeremy Corbyn was heavily criticised by traditional media during the 2017 election.
■ Social media is increasingly important.
■ In 2017, Labour's online campaign increased its vote share.

Factors influencing the outcome of elections

The following factors can influence the outcome of elections:

■ leadership
■ funding
■ policies
■ record in government
■ media response
■ election campaign
■ electoral system

The impact of minor parties

Minor parties can have a significant impact on political debates and the political agenda.

Synoptic link

Attempts to limit party spending and funding in the USA have been limited by constitutional rulings that they undermine free speech and free expression, leading to American elections costing billions, while UK elections are in the millions.

Exam tip

You will need examples for each of the factors that influence the outcome of elections (see the election case studies in 2.2 Elections and referendums).

Key term

Political agenda The political issues that are prioritised by political parties, the media, or in general public debate.

Table 51 **The impact of minor parties**

Party	Impact on political debates and political agenda
Scottish National Party (SNP)	■ 2014 Scottish independence referendum ■ Landslide victory in Scotland in the 2015 general election made it third largest party in UK Parliament ■ Criticised UK government for ignoring Scotland in Brexit negotiations ■ Called for second EU referendum and another Scottish independence referendum
UK Independence Party (UKIP)	■ Successfully campaigned for a referendum on EU membership ■ Reduced significance since 2016 EU referendum
Plaid Cymru	■ Clear voice for Wales ■ Limited impact as it is a small party
Democratic Unionist Party (DUP)	■ Power sharing in Northern Ireland ■ Supported minority Conservative government from 2017 ■ Blocked Theresa May's EU withdrawal agreement because of impact on Northern Ireland
Green Party	■ Limited direct influence because of its size ■ Other progressive parties developed environmental policies to compete for 'green' votes
Brexit Party	■ Formed 2019 to show continued demand for Brexit ■ Won 2019 European Parliament elections ■ Aims to pressure Conservatives and Labour by attracting their voters
Independent Group for Change	■ Formed 2019 to promote centrist policies ■ Comprised of 11 breakaway Labour and Conservative MPs ■ Came seventh in the 2019 European Parliament elections and failed to win any seats: six of its MPs left the party as a result

Party systems

Table 52 **Different** party systems

Single-party	■ Only one party exists and has total control
Dominant party	■ One party dominates the system, though others exist, e.g. Labour in the Welsh Assembly
Two-party	■ Two parties have a chance of gaining power ■ Typical product of FPTP ■ Only a Conservative or a Labour leader has a realistic chance of winning a UK election
Two-and-a-half-party	■ Two main parties and a significant minor party which will act as 'king-maker' ■ Liberal Democrats occupied this position during coalition 2010–15

Multi-party	■ Many parties have a chance of gaining power through coalitions
	■ Typical product of proportional voting systems
	■ Increased role of minor parties in UK in recent years:
	  □ DUP supported Conservative minority government from 2017
	  □ Coalition with Liberal Democrats 2010–15
	  □ SNP, Sinn Fein and DUP in government in devolved nations (though power sharing suspended in Northern Ireland from 2017)
	  □ UKIP victory in 2014 European Parliament elections prompted Conservatives to include an EU referendum in its 2015 manifesto
	  □ Brexit Party won 2019 European Parliament elections, Liberal Democrats came second

Key term

Party system Political system defined by the number of parties that competitively contest elections. Different electoral systems produce different party systems.

Exam tip

You need to recognise that the UK has been developing towards a multi-party system in recent years and be able to analyse and evaluate the extent to which it remains a two-party system.

Do you know?

1 What is a political party?
2 What do political parties do?
3 How do the main parties relate to ideologies?
4 How are the main parties structured?
5 What are the arguments for and against state funding of parties?
6 How does the media interact with parties?
7 What impact have minor parties had on UK politics?
8 How is the UK developing towards a multi-party system?

Synoptic link

The success of parties and the nature of the party system often comes down to how parties are perceived through their portrayal in the media.

2.4 Pressure groups

You need to know

- what a pressure group is
- different types of groups
- methods used by pressure groups
- factors affecting pressure group influence
- links to political parties, government and the media
- how other groups influence Parliament and government
- the impact of pressure groups on democracy

Types of group

Key pressure group distinctions:
- interest vs promotional
- insider vs outsider

Key terms

Pressure groups Organisations that attempt to put pressure on those in power to achieve their aims.

Interest groups Groups that campaign for their own interests.

Promotional groups Groups that campaign for a cause on behalf of others.

Insider groups Groups consulted by the government so have 'insider status'.

Outsider groups Groups not consulted by the government have 'outsider status'.

Exam tips

- None of the group distinctions are perfect, and many groups have elements of both: the British Medical Association (BMA) will promote public health issues (promotional) but also campaign for the interests of doctors (interest).
- Insider/outsider status of pressure groups can change depending on the government.

Pressure group methods

Table 53 **Pressure group methods**

Methods	Examples
Conventional	■ Publicity campaigns ■ Lobbying ■ Petitions ■ Legal challenges
Direct action	■ Demonstrations ■ Marches ■ Publicity stunts ■ Strikes ■ Civil disobedience

Pressure group case studies

Table 54 **Pressure group case studies**

Group	Successes	Lack of success
BMA (insider group)	Lobbied the government to ban work-place smoking in 2007	New junior doctors' contract imposed by government, despite BMA lobbying and 2016 strike
Greenpeace (outsider group)	Growing political consensus that low carbon economy is needed	Direct action methods criticised, and government environmental policy is limited

Pressure group influence

Pressure groups aim to influence politics. The following factors determine how successful they are:

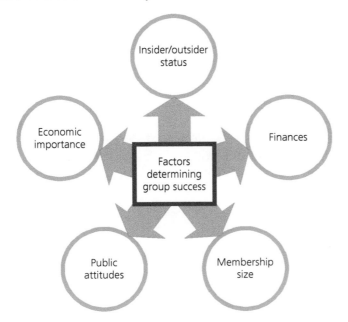

Figure 17 **Factors determining group success**

Other influences on government and Parliament

Think tanks:

■ develop policy ideas
■ research key areas
■ promote a sectional agenda

Lobbyists:

■ are groups with personal connections to those in power
■ are hired by other groups to gain access to those in power
■ seek to persuade those in power on behalf of other people (who pay)

Corporations:

■ are big businesses and financial organisations
■ control an important sector of the economy
■ seek favourable legislation and government action
■ can threaten to relocate to pressure the government

Media:

■ reporting influences how the public view the pressure group and its cause
■ help to set the political agenda

Key terms

Think tanks Groups that are privately funded to research and develop policy ideas.

Lobbyists People hired to persuade those in power.

Synoptic link

Think tanks have replaced the party function of policy formulation in recent years.

Exam tip

You need to evaluate how these other types of groups influence government and Parliament.

Are pressure groups good for democracy?

Table 55 **Are pressure groups good for democracy?**

Yes	No
■ Promote pluralism ■ Allow focus on a specific issue ■ Participation between elections ■ Large memberships ■ Provide information to government ■ Minimum turnout of 50% required in strike ballots to prevent unions striking with little support	■ Elitism if groups are dominated by powerful people ■ Pressure groups can lack internal democracy ■ Unaccountable to the electorate ■ Can prevent joined-up government ■ Violent direct action is unlawful ■ New Right argue that striking undermines the democratic state

Key terms

Pluralism Different groups compete equally for power and influence.

Elitism Powerful elites dominate society and government.

Do you know?

1 What is a pressure group?
2 What are the main four different types of groups?
3 What methods are used by pressure groups?
4 What factors affect pressure group influence?
5 How do pressure groups link to political parties, government and the media?
6 What other groups influence Parliament and government?
7 Why are pressure groups important in a pluralist society?

2.5 The European Union (EU)

You need to know

- the aims of the EU
- the role and functions of the EU
- key EU institutions
- the impact of the EU on the UK
- the reasons for and impact of Brexit

Aims of the EU

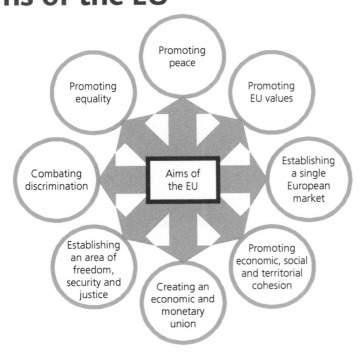

Figure 18 **Aims of the EU**

The values of the EU include:

- human dignity
- freedom
- democracy
- equality
- the rule of law
- respect for human rights

The single market is based on the four freedoms; free movement of goods, services, people and capital. Within this, the EU has the eurozone, comprised of 19 members who all share the same currency.

EU institutions

There are five key EU institutions:

- European Commission
- Council of the European Union
- European Council
- European Parliament
- Court of Justice of the European Union

The European Commission

Commissioners are nominated by national governments and approved by the European Parliament.

The Commission:

- initiates draft legislation
- executes EU legislation
- administers EU spending
- represents the EU internationally

The Council of the European Union

The Council of the European Union is made up of ministers chosen by and representing the 28 member states. Decisions must be made either unanimously or by qualified majority voting (55% of member states representing 65% of the EU population).

The Council of the European Union:

- shares legislative powers with the European Parliament
- coordinates economic policy
- develops the EU's foreign and security policies

Exam tip

You need to be able to analyse and evaluate the extent to which the EU has achieved its aims.

Synoptic link

The values of the EU relate closely to the democracy section of the course.

Exam tip

The European Court of Justice only deals with EU law. Cases about the European Convention of Human Rights are dealt with in the European Court of Human Rights, which is not part of the EU.

The European Council

The European Council is made up of the member states' heads of government or heads of states and their foreign ministers, meeting four times a year.

The European Council:
- discusses major issues
- sets the EU's political direction
- makes decisions on EU foreign and economic policy
- agrees to treaty changes
- launches new initiatives

The European Parliament

The European Parliament is made up of 751 MEPs elected every 5 years by EU citizens. Seats are allocated proportionately.

The European Parliament:
- legislates (but cannot initiate legislation)
- authorises and amends the EU budget
- gives democratic legitimacy to appointed elements
- scrutinises the work of the other branches

Key term

MEP Member of the European Parliament.

Synoptic link

As the only elected element is the EU Parliament, people question the democratic legitimacy of the EU.

The Court of Justice of the European Union

Based in Luxembourg, the Court is a final court of appeal for cases relating to EU law, institutions, business and individuals.

The Court of Justice:
- clarifies EU law for member states
- makes rulings on areas of conflict or uncertainty

The EU and UK

Agreeing to be in the EU meant accepting EU law into British law. This placed restrictions on UK sovereignty by:
- accepting the primacy of EU law
- giving courts the power to suspend statute law incompatible with EU law
- banning independent trade agreements

In theory, many of these powers will return to the UK after Brexit.

The main areas of difficulty between the UK and EU concerned:
- the Common Agricultural Policy
- the Common Fisheries Policy
- the EU budget and the UK's contribution
- the Social Chapter and workers' rights
- immigration and the free movement of labour

The decision to leave the EU

In June 2016 the UK held a referendum on EU membership. A majority (52% : 48%) voted to leave, triggering the process of Brexit.

Reasons why people voted to leave included:
- the loss of sovereignty to the EU
- concerns over EU policies
- concerns about immigration
- popular nationalism
- popular Euroscepticism
- concerns about the cost of EU membership

Impact of Brexit on UK politics

- David Cameron and Theresa May both resigned as prime minister because of Brexit.
- Minority government: May lost her majority after calling the 2017 snap general election over Brexit, and Boris Johnson was left without a working majority after removing the Conservative whip from 21 MPs who defied him over Brexit.
- Conflict between Parliament and government: Parliament refused to approve May's Brexit deal and voted to prevent Johnson from leaving without a deal.
- New parties: the Brexit Party and the Independent Group for Change were formed.
- Election results: the pro-leave Brexit Party won the European Parliament elections in June 2019, with the pro-remain Liberal Democrats in second place, showing the public remained divided.

Synoptic link

Brexit creates challenges for devolution. While the UK voted to leave, Scotland and Northern Ireland voted to remain. The Scottish Parliament and the Welsh Assembly both oppose a no-deal Brexit. Northern Ireland's DUP has refused to support May's withdrawal agreement because it could lead to Northern Ireland being treated differently to the rest of the UK.

Exam tip

You need to be able to analyse and evaluate the impact of the EU on UK politics and policy making.

Do you know?

1 What are the main aims of the EU?

2 What are the four freedoms of the single market?

3 What are the main institutions of the EU, and what powers do they have?

4 Which areas have seen conflict between the UK and EU?

5 Why did the UK vote to leave the EU?

End of section 2 questions

1 What are the differences between direct and representative democracy?

2 How do elections promote democracy?

3 Are pressure group politics beneficial to UK democracy?

4 What are the key differences in policies between the major parties?

5 What are the main divisions within the political parties?

6 How are different parties affected by FPTP?

7 Are party leaders more important than party policy?

8 Does party politics help or hinder UK democracy?

9 Is the use of referendums beneficial to representative democracy?

10 Why was 1997 a watershed election?

11 How does insider or outsider status affect a pressure group's influence?

12 Do pressure groups benefit UK democracy?

13 Has the EU been successful?

14 Why did the UK vote to leave the EU?

15 How significant an impact has the EU had on UK policy?

3 US politics

3.1 The US Constitution

You need to know

- the nature of the US Constitution
- the significance of constitutional principles
- how the federal system of government works
- how the Constitution is amended
- how the Constitution protects civil liberties and rights

Nature of the US Constitution

The US Constitution has three key features:

- It is codified, meaning in one single, authoritative document.
- It is entrenched, meaning it is difficult to amend.
- It has many vague elements, opening it up to interpretation.

As a result of these features, the US Constitution is a higher form of law than other laws.

Key terms

Constitution A set of formal laws to govern a country.

Codified When laws are gathered into one single document.

Entrenched When laws are entrenched, they are difficult to overturn and amend.

Synoptic links

- As constitutional law is higher than laws made by Congress, the US Supreme Court can strike down statute laws, unlike the UK Supreme Court.
- The debates over powers and the relationship between the branches and the federal government and the states depend on interpretations of the Constitution.

Amendments

The US Constitution has been amended (changed) 27 times since it was written.

Any amendment must go through two stages: proposal and ratification.

Table 56 **The amendment process**

Proposed by...	■ Two-thirds of BOTH houses of Congress (the House and the Senate) **or** ■ Legislatures in two-thirds of the states calling for a National Constitutional Convention
Ratified by...	■ Three-quarters of state legislatures (38) **or** ■ Ratifying conventions in three-quarters of the states

Table 57 Advantages and disadvantages of the amendment process

Advantages	Disadvantages
■ Any amendment will have the support of a clear majority of the US ■ Pointless or needless amendments are not passed ■ It preserves the sanctity of the US Constitution ■ The role of the states in ratification retains federalism	■ As so few amendments are passed, the unelected Supreme Court has too much power in making 'interpretative amendments' ■ Desirable or necessary amendments cannot be made ■ It allows the Constitution to become outdated ■ Many amendments fail to be ratified by the states, e.g. the Equal Rights Amendment (ERA)

The Bill of Rights

The first ten amendments are known as 'the Bill of Rights'. This aims to protect citizens and states from the federal government.

Table 58 The Bill of Rights

Amendment	Rights
I	Freedom of religion, speech, petition, press and assembly
II	Right to bear arms
III	No quartering of troops in private homes
IV	Unreasonable stop and searches
V	Rights of the accused
VI	Right to trial by jury
VII	Common law
VIII	Cruel and unusual punishments
IX	Protection of unenumerated rights
X	Powers reserved to the states (federalism)

Principles of the US Constitution

Aims of the Founding Fathers:

- democracy
- limited government
- federalism
- national government

The key principles of the US Constitution are:

- separation of powers
- checks and balances
- bipartisanship
- limited government
- federalism

Separation of powers

- The different branches of the federal government are separated.
- They physically occupy different locations and people cannot be in two branches at once.
- Different branches have different powers, but powers are in fact shared, while it is institutions that are separate.

Synoptic link

This is the formal process of amending the Constitution, but the Supreme Court amends it whenever it applies judicial review, meaning the Constitution is effectively amended several times a year.

Key terms

Founding Fathers Influential political figures from the era of the American revolution and creation of the USA. Most often used to describe the men who wrote the Constitution.

Principle A central idea or belief.

Separation of powers When there is a distinct separation between the executive, legislative and judicial branches of government.

Checks and balances System whereby the different branches have powers divided between them and to oversee each other.

Table 59 **Separated powers**

President	Congress	Supreme Court
Power to enforce laws	Power to make and pass laws	Power to review laws
Power to nominate	Power of confirmation	Power to determine constitutionality
Power to spend	Power to tax	Power to determine constitutionality

Checks and balances

The separation of powers means power is distributed between the branches so that no single branch can become too powerful. Each branch acts as a check on the other two to prevent any form of dictatorship.

Table 60 **Checks in the US Constitution**

Checks by/on	The president	Congress	The Supreme Court
The president		■ Veto a Bill	■ Pardon
Congress	■ Overriding a veto ■ Confirmation of appointments and treaties ■ Impeachment		■ Proposing constitutional amendments ■ Impeachment
The Supreme Court	■ Declaring actions unconstitutional	■ Striking down unconstitutional laws	

Bipartisanship

- ■ The Founding Fathers believed a separation of powers would force factions to compromise to create better legislation.
- ■ Divided government can occur between the executive and legislative branches.
- ■ While the Constitution can promote bipartisanship and compromise, it can also lead to less effective government.
- ■ Partisan groups use checks and balances to block their rivals.

Table 61 **Recent periods of divided and unified government**

Years	Presidency	House	Senate
2019+	Republican	Democrat	Republican
2017–19	Republican	Republican	Republican
2015–17	Democrat	Republican	Republican
2011–15	Democrat	Republican	Democrat
2009–11	Democrat	Democrat	Democrat
2007–09	Republican	Democrat	Democrat
2003–07	Republican	Republican	Republican
2001–03	Republican	Republican	Democrat

Key terms

Divided government
When the presidency is controlled by a different party from one or both chambers of Congress.

Bipartisanship When two parties cooperate and compromise.

Limited government

The separation of powers, and checks and balances were designed to limit the power of the national or 'federal' government.

The Bill of Rights was introduced to ensure the power of the government was limited.

Federalism

A strong national government was seen as necessary in 1788, but states wanted to retain their own powers and customs:

■ The Constitution created a federal system.
■ The national (or federal) government would be strong, but limited, with enumerated powers over some areas.
■ State governments would hold power and authority over all other areas.

However, as America changed, so did the nature of federalism, with implied powers being used to give more power to the federal government at the expense of the states.

Federalism since 1968

Federalism increased because:

■ New federalism gave more control to the states with block grants.
■ Reagan attempted to reduce the size of the federal government.
■ Supreme Court rulings, like *US* vs *Lopez*, began to limit the power of the federal government.

However, under Bush and Obama federalism decreased in key areas:

■ **education:** No Child Left Behind and Rise to the Top
■ **healthcare:** Medicare expansion and the Affordable Care Act
■ **defence:** Homeland Security and increasing terror threats
■ **economic:** bailouts and growing federal employment
■ **environment:** the growth of the Environmental Protection Agency (EPA) and environmental initiatives

Federalism in the Constitution

Evidence of states' rights and powers in the Constitution include:

■ Representation is to be determined by each state.
■ All states get equal representation in the Senate.
■ Representatives must reside in their state.
■ Electoral processes are to be determined by the states.
■ The Electoral College is based on state representation.
■ Right to levy state taxes.

Key terms

Limited government The powers of the government are restricted by constitutional laws and rights.

Federalism The idea that power is shared between a national government and state governments.

Enumerated powers Powers expressly granted to the federal government in the Constitution.

Implied powers Powers that are open to interpretation.

Exam tip

Before the Civil War (1861–65) the USA was described in the plural (the United States are); after the Civil War it was described in the singular (the United States is) showing a change in federalism.

Synoptic link

Through devolution the UK appears to have federalism, but the rights of devolved bodies are granted by Parliament and not protected by the Constitution, so their power is much weaker than in the USA.

- State governors fill vacancies.
- Each state must respect the laws and customs of the others.
- Ratification was to be determined by the state.
- Ratification of amendments is determined by states.
- The 10th Amendment.

Debates about the Constitution

Does the Constitution work today?

The Constitution was written in the eighteenth century and there has been debate about whether it is still fit for contemporary US government as shown in Table 62.

Table 62 **Does the Constitution work today?**

Yes	No
■ Codified in a single document so citizens know the framework by which the USA is governed ■ Widely revered and respected ■ Can be amended to give modern updates as required, e.g. women given the vote in the 19th Amendment (1920)	■ Gives too much power to the unelected Supreme Court justices who interpret it ■ The most divisive issues in US politics focus on the Constitution, e.g. abortion, gun control ■ Amendment process has prevented popular changes, e.g. gun control

Does the Constitution protect civil liberties and rights effectively?

Table 63 **Does the Constitution protect civil liberties and rights effectively?**

Yes	No
■ Rights are entrenched within the Constitution ■ Bill of Rights gives citizens key rights ■ Codified constitution allows US citizens to have a clear understanding of their rights ■ Supreme Court decisions have increased rights, e.g. abortion, same-sex marriage	■ Wording of rights can be vague, e.g. the 8th Amendment prohibits 'cruel and unusual' punishments ■ Opponents of the 2nd Amendment argue 'right to bear arms' was given in the eighteenth century but is outdated ■ Amendment process makes it too difficult to update the Constitution with new rights ■ Supreme Court judges have too much power in interpreting rights

UK/US comparison

Table 64 **The US Constitution and UK constitution compared**

US	UK
Codified	Uncodified
Rigid	Flexible
Federal	Unitary
Constitutional sovereignty	Parliamentary sovereignty
Entrenched rights	Unentrenched rights
Separation of powers	Fusion of powers (legislature and executive only)
Strong judiciary	Weak judiciary

Do you know?

1 What are the aims and principles of the Constitution?

2 How can the Constitution be amended?

3 How has federalism in the USA changed?

4 How does the Constitution protect civil liberties and rights?

5 What are the similarities and differences between the US Constitution and UK constitution?

3.2 Congress

You need to know

■ the structure of Congress

■ the powers of both chambers in Congress

■ the composition of Congress

■ the functions of Congress

■ the effectiveness of Congress

■ the importance of the party system and committee system

■ the role of senators and representatives

Structure of Congress

Overview

Congress is bicameral, meaning it has two chambers:

■ the House of Representatives (the lower chamber)

■ the Senate (the upper chamber)

Table 65 Features of the House of Representatives and the Senate

Features of the House of Representatives	Features of the Senate
■ 435 members called 'representatives' ■ Each represents a district ■ Representatives are allocated based on population ■ Each state must have at least one representative ■ Districts are reapportioned every 10 years ■ Representatives are elected for 2-year terms ■ They must be over 25 ■ They must have been a citizen for 7 years ■ They must reside in the state they represent ■ A number of non-voting representatives speak on behalf of American territories ■ House elects its own Speaker	■ 100 members called 'senators' ■ Each represents a state ■ Each state has two senators, regardless of size ■ Senators have 6-year terms ■ They must be over 30 ■ They must have been a citizen for 9 years ■ They must reside in the state they represent ■ The vice president of the USA is the President of the Senate (Chair) ■ The Vice President rarely chairs the Senate: this is usually done by the President *pro tempore* of the Senate (the most senior member of the majority party in the Senate)

The committee system

Key terms

Committee chair The chairperson of a committee who has power over the agenda and appointment of sub-committees.

Standing committee A permanent policy committee, often linked to a government department.

Synoptic link

The structure of Congress is set out in Article 1 of the Constitution. Any changes would require a constitutional amendment.

Synoptic link

The US standing committees are similar to the UK's select committees.

Although major votes take place on the floor of each chamber, most of the real work is done in Congress's various committees, headed by powerful committee chairs.

Table 66 Key congressional committees

Committee	Definition	Membership	Key details
Standing committees	Linked to government departments on a specific policy area	Senate: 18 House: 30–40	■ Determine whether or not to pass a Bill to the full chamber ■ Conduct investigations into its policy area ■ Hold hearings and determine whether or not to pass presidential nominees to the full chamber (Senate only)

The House Rules Committee	Determine rules regarding amendments to legislation and the order they are presented to the House	13–15, House only	■ Allocate key rules:
			  □ open rules — unlimited amendments
			  □ modified rules — limits on the number of amendments, who can propose them and where they can go
			  □ closed rules — no amendments allowed

Committee	Definition	Membership	Key details
Conference committees	Ad hoc committees designed to reconcile differences between House and Senate versions of a piece of legislation	Members come from each chamber	<ul><li>Agree a final version of a Bill</li><li>Once a final version of a Bill is agreed in a conference committee it will be sent back to each chamber for a final vote</li><li>If it is rejected by either chamber, it may be sent back to the conference committee or can be sent back to the original standing committee</li></ul>
Select committees	Investigative committees for issues beyond one standing committee	Various	<ul><li>Most are ad hoc, but there are five permanent select committees:</li><li>Senate — Aging, Ethics, Indian affairs, Intelligence</li><li>House — Intelligence</li></ul>

Party system

The party system in Congress has the following features:
- It is a two-party system.
- Republicans belong to the House or Senate Republican caucus.
- Democrats belong to the House or Senate Democratic caucus.
- Each party caucus elects a leader to coordinate the party in the House or the Senate.
- Party discipline is weak.

Congressional caucuses

Although dominated by the main parties, Congress is sub-divided into congressional caucuses. Members of Congress may belong to several different caucuses.

Caucuses:
- provide information to members on legislation and policy
- support each other in promoting a specific goal
- collaborate to promote an agenda

Key caucuses include:
- the Congressional Black Caucus
- the Congressional Hispanic Caucus
- the Congressional Hispanic Conference
- the House Freedom Caucus
- the Tuesday Group

Exam tip

As much of the work of Congress is done in committee, it is important to reference them in any assessment of congressional power or effectiveness.

Key term

Congressional caucuses Discussion groups that meet to discuss a shared interest or concern. These can be party based, or bipartisan.

Composition of Congress

Table 67 **The composition of the 116th Congress (2019–)**

Party	■ House — Democrat majority ■ Senate — Republican majority
Average age	59 years
Women	A record high: ■ 24% of representatives in the House ■ 25% of senators
People of colour:	21% of Congress (a record)
■ African–Americans	■ 10% of Congress
■ Hispanic–Americans	■ 8% of Congress
■ Native–Americans	■ Four members of the House (a record)
■ Professional background	■ Dominated by politics, business and law
Religious faith	■ 88% Christian ■ 6% Jewish ■ Three Muslim members ■ Three Hindus ■ Two Buddhists

Powers of Congress
Concurrent powers

The following powers are held by both the House and the Senate:

- legislation: any law must pass both chambers
- power of the purse
- power to investigate the executive branch
- overriding a presidential veto; must pass by 2/3 majority in both chambers
- initiating constitutional amendments — 2/3 majority in each chamber
- the impeachment process
- declaring war
- confirmation of an appointed vice president

Exclusive powers of the House

- beginning consideration of money Bills
- initiating an impeachment
- electing the president if there is no majority in the Electoral College

---

Key term

Power of the purse Only Congress can impose federal taxes on people. Tax Bills start in the House but can be amended by the Senate. Both chambers must approve the budget in order for it to become law. Congress can put pressure on the executive by refusing to pass its budget, as this would cause a government shutdown.

Synoptic link

Impeachment is an important constitutional check on the executive. In September 2019, Democrat Nancy Pelosi, the Speaker of the House of Representatives, launched an inquiry over whether to impeach President Trump.

Exclusive powers of the Senate

- confirming presidential appointments to the Cabinet, judiciary and ambassadorships
- ratifying treaties
- trying cases of impeachment
- electing the vice president if there is no majority in the Electoral College

Functions of Congress

Representation

The frequency of elections, the growth in congressional primaries and the weakness of the US party system mean representatives and senators are much more engaged with their constituents than British MPs.

Representatives will engage with constituents by:
- holding 'town hall' meetings
- meeting with individual constituents
- making formal visits
- appearing on local media
- press interviews
- addressing popular groups

In representing constituents, representatives will:
- vote on legislation
- work on committees that deal with local interests
- help constituents with federal issues
- gain pork for their area through pork barrel policies

Factors that affect congressional voting include:
- **The 'folks back home':** constituent demands and needs.
- **The political party:** its ideology, position or assistance.
- **The administration:** the president may seek to persuade representatives.
- **Pressure groups:** groups will lobby for beneficial legislation.
- **Colleagues:** senior colleagues will often advise or lobby others.
- **Staff:** congressional staff will give advice on legislation.
- **Personal beliefs:** some representatives follow their conscience.

> **Exam tip**
>
> Be prepared to analyse and evaluate the relevant strengths of the House of Representatives and the Senate.

> **Synoptic link**
>
> The weakness of the US party systems gives constituents greater control over their representatives.

> **Exam tip**
>
> If you are asked whether representation in the USA is effective, improve your answer by analysing both the trustee model (where representatives are entrusted to make decisions in the national interest) and the delegate model (where representatives simply do as their constituents instruct).

> **Key term**
>
> Pork barrel Describes funds given to benefit a congressional district.

> **Synoptic link**
>
> Voting records are publicised by pressure groups to put pressure on a representative to vote the way their constituents want.

Legislation

Table 68 assesses the extent to which Congress passes legislation effectively.

Table 68 **Does Congress pass legislation effectively?**

Yes	No
■ The approval of both chambers is needed, so all new laws have been agreed by both Senate and House ■ Weak party discipline means that bipartisan support is often needed to pass legislation, encouraging cooperation between parties ■ Power of the purse requires both chambers to approve the budget. This keeps a check on executive spending	■ Only 2–3% of Bills become law ■ Gridlock often occurs in times of divided government ■ Use of filibusters allows individual senators to 'kill off' legislation ■ Presidential vetoes are rarely overturned as a super-majority is needed (2/3 of both the House and the Senate) ■ Government shutdowns can happen if Congress refuses to pass a budget

Oversight

To scrutinise the work of the executive branch, Congress can:
- use the power of subpoena to gain access to documents and testimony
- hold individuals in contempt
- investigate and confirm presidential nominees
- appoint a special investigator

Much of the work of oversight is done by the standing committees. Members of the executive branch regularly have to attend questions from the relevant standing committee or a select committee.

Congressional oversight is most effective when:
- there is divided government
- Congress is more popular than the president
- it is non-partisan

Criticism has emerged of oversight being used on a partisan basis to simply oppose the president, particularly with confirmations.

Congress can also oversee the Supreme Court by holding hearings and votes in the Senate on Supreme Court nominees and can bring impeachment cases against federal judges who fail in their duties.

Key terms

Filibuster The Senate process of using procedures and debates to delay business until a measure is dropped.

Subpoena A legal writ demanding that people are, or material is, presented to a body.

Non-partisan Non-partisan politicians do not allow party politics to affect their conduct.

Synoptic link

Unlike the Houses of Parliament, the executive has no formal presence in Congress, meaning Congress is freer to investigate the executive.

Exam tips

- You need to analyse and evaluate the relationship of Congress to the executive, including the power of the purse, the presidential veto, and the significance of divided government.
- You also need to analyse and evaluate Congress' relationship with the Supreme Court, including the Senate's role in confirming judicial nominees, and the Court's judicial review of Congress' laws.

US/UK comparison

Table 69 **A comparison of Parliament and Congress**

Parliament	Congress
Bicameral (Commons and Lords)	Bicameral (House and Senate)
Executive is present	Executive is absent
Strong party discipline	Weak party discipline
Limited number of Bills introduced	Vast number of Bills introduced
Agenda set by the government	Congress sets its own agenda
Unequal powers	Equal power across the chambers
Sovereign	Bound by the Constitution
No approval of appointments	Approves some presidential nominees
Undemocratic elements	Democratic
Executive questioned by Commons	Executive members questioned by committee

Do you know?

1 What are the shared and separate powers of each chamber?
2 What are the roles and functions of Congress?
3 What is the composition of Congress in terms of age, gender, race, religion and professional background?
4 How does the party system work?
5 What are the different types of congressional committees?
6 How do senators and representatives represent their constituents?

3.3 The presidency

You need to know

- the sources of the powers of the president
- the difference between the formal and informal powers of the president
- constraints on presidential powers
- what the Cabinet and Executive Office of the President (EXOP) do
- the relationship between the presidency and other institutions
- an example of the waxing and waning of presidential power
- why there is debate about whether the presidency is 'imperial' or 'imperilled'

Formal powers of the president

The Constitution is an important source of presidential power, allowing the president to:

- propose legislation
- submit an annual budget
- sign or veto legislation
- act as the chief executive
- nominate executive branch officials
- nominate federal judges
- to act as commander-in-chief
- negotiate treaties
- issue pardons
- perform the duties of head of state

As head of government the president must oversee the day-to-day running of the federal government. As head of state, the president acts as a spokesperson and leader for the whole nation.

Key term

Executive The branch of government that takes action: the government.

Synoptic link

In the USA the roles of head of government and head of state are combined in one person, but in the UK, they are separated between the monarch (head of state) and the prime minister (head of government).

Table 70 **Examples of formal powers being used**

President	Power	Detail
Bush	Head of state	9/11 Attacks, Hurricane Katrina
Bush	Commander-in-chief	War on terror, Afghanistan, Iraq
Obama	Propose legislation	Patient Protection and Affordable Care Act, 2010
Obama	Nominate federal judges	Sotomayor, Kagin, Garland
Obama	Negotiate treaties	Trans-Pacific Partnership, Iran deal
Trump	Nominate federal judges	Gorsuch, Kavanaugh
Trump	Sign legislation	Tax Cuts and Jobs Act, 2017
Trump	Nominate executive branch official	DeVos, Tillerson, Kelly

- **Enumerated powers** of the president are set out in Article II of the Constitution.
- **Inherent powers** of the president are not specifically set out in the Constitution, but are required for the president to carry out the role as chief executive of the government.

Informal powers of the president

The president also has informal powers which are not in the Constitution as shown in Table 71.

Table 71 **Informal power of the president**

Informal power	Source	Detail
De facto leaders of their party	Electoral mandate	▪ In effect presidents act as head of their party
Powers of persuasion	Electoral mandate, role as leader of the nation	▪ Can use influence to win support of other political figures
Agenda setting	Role as leader of the nation	▪ Presidents' priorities are at the top of the political agenda
World leader	Role as leader of the nation	▪ International influence
Direct authority and stretching of implied powers	Role as chief executive	▪ Executive orders ▪ Signing statements ▪ Recess appointments ▪ Executive agreements
Bureaucratic powers	Role as chief executive	▪ Control the Executive Office of the President (EXOP)

Leader of the nation

The presidency (along with the vice presidency) is the only office to be elected on a national basis. This electoral mandate gives the president greater authority when claiming to represent the nation and provide leadership.

The larger the Electoral College victory, the stronger a president's mandate:

- Presidents who receive more than 50% of the popular vote have a stronger mandate and generally find it easier to convince Congress to pass their legislation.
- Presidents who win the Electoral College but lose the popular vote are seen to have a weaker mandate and carry less authority with Congress, e.g. President Donald Trump.

Key terms

Electoral mandate The authority given by winning an election.

Powers of persuasion The ability to persuade politicians or the public to support a point of view.

Executive orders Legal documents instructing federal officials on how to carry out certain functions and what actions to take.

Signing statements A statement that some part of a law being signed by the president will not be enforced for constitutional reasons.

Recess appointment An appointment made to a federal office while the Senate is not in session. The appointment only lasts until the end of the following Senate session.

Executive agreements Bilateral agreements with foreign nations that do not have the same status as formal treaties.

Executive Office of the President (EXOP) A group of about a dozen agencies that support the president in running the federal government.

Chief executive

As head of the government presidents have the power to determine:
- how laws are to be implemented
- how funds are allocated
- which cases to prosecute
- how to use direct authority powers to allow them to govern

Modern developments

During the twentieth century presidents developed their informal powers by:
- stretching their implied powers to increase their executive authority
- issuing more executive orders and signing statements
- making more executive agreements with foreign countries, rather than treaties
- increasing the size and importance of EXOP

> **Key term**
>
> Implied powers **Powers suggested by the Constitution, but not explicitly stated.**

Constraints on the president's powers

While all presidents have the same constitutional powers, their ability to use these powers depends on a number of criteria.

Table 72 **Factors affecting presidential power**

Factor	Detail
Electoral mandate	A stronger mandate makes it easier to persuade
Public approval	Stronger approval makes it easier to persuade
Party support in Congress	A supportive Congress is more likely to support a legislative agenda and confirm appointments. This is easier with unified government rather than divided government
Orientation of the Supreme Court	The Supreme Court may be more or less willing to strike down executive actions depending on whether it has a liberal or conservative majority
Term	Presidents become weaker as their terms progress, particularly in their second term
Media and public opinion	The media's view of presidents helps to shape the public's opinion of them
Crises	Major crises can rally public and political support behind presidents, making it easier to achieve their goals. However, a badly handled crisis can damage a president's reputation

▶

Factor	Detail
Formal checks and balances: the use of any of these can limit presidential power	Checks by Congress on the president: ■ amending, delaying or rejecting the president's legislation ■ overriding a presidential veto (rarely used as needs a 2/3 majority in both chambers of Congress) ■ power of the purse (can lead to government shutdown) ■ Senate can refuse to confirm presidential appointments (e.g. Obama's nominee to the Supreme Court, Merrick Garland) ■ Senate can refuse to ratify treaties (rarely happens, needs a 2/3 majority and presidents can use executive agreements instead) ■ power to declare war (not used since 1941) ■ investigation of the executive ■ impeachment and trial of the president (rarely used, but Bill Clinton was tried and acquitted in 1998) Checks by the judiciary on the president: ■ judicial review

Relationship between the presidency and other institutions

Cabinet

Members of the Cabinet are appointed by the president to run a federal department.

■ Cabinet members are policy specialists.
■ Cabinet members may be former politicians, academics or experts in their field.
■ Cabinet tends to meet a few times a year: the frequency depends on the president's wishes.
■ Under President Obama the Cabinet met on average 3.5 times a year, compared to 6 times a year under President George W. Bush.
■ Presidents do not have to take the advice of their Cabinet members: the Constitution gives the president sole executive authority.

Cabinet remains important, but its advisory role has largely been replaced by EXOP.

Executive Office of the President (EXOP)

EXOP is the collective name for the heads of key executive agencies who advise and assist the president in running the executive branch. EXOP is based in the 'West Wing' of the White House.

EXOP was created and grew because of the increase in:
■ the role of the federal government
■ the size and diversity of America
■ the USA's international involvement

Synoptic link

The factors affecting presidential power are similar in many ways to factors affecting prime ministerial power, although UK prime ministers do not have term limits and have a different system of checks and balances.

Table 73 **The key EXOP departments**

The White House Office (WHO)	The Office of Management and Budget (OMB)	The National Security Council (NSC)
■ Headed by the chief of staff ■ Organises the president's schedule ■ Grants access to the president (in person or through communications) ■ Gives public/press statements ■ Organises events	■ Advises the allocation of federal funds ■ Oversees federal spending ■ Approves executive policy proposals	■ Advises on foreign and military actions ■ Coordinates information from various departments and agencies ■ Can be used as an alternative to the State Department

Federal bureaucracy and federal agencies

The federal bureaucracy is made up of:

- government departments headed by a Cabinet officer e.g. the Department of State
- independently run federal agencies, e.g. the Central Intelligence Agency (CIA)

Republican presidents generally aim to reduce the size of the federal bureaucracy, while Democrat presidents often increase it.

> **Exam tip**
>
> The Cabinet is made up of departments, but EXOP is made up of agencies, offices and councils, which are less formal than departments.

Waxing and waning of presidential power

- Presidencies tend to grow more powerful before gradually losing power.
- This is known as 'waxing and waning', a reference to the changing size of the moon over a lunar month.
- Obama's presidency began with a historic victory in 2008 when he was elected the first black US president.
- Democrats controlled both Houses of Congress, so Obama was able to pass an economic stimulus and his signature 'Obamacare' healthcare policy.
- Although he was re-elected in 2012, the Republicans won the House in 2010 and the Senate in 2014
- In his final 2 years Obama struggled to pass his legislation through Congress and increasingly relied on executive orders to get things done.

Imperial or imperilled presidency?

Table 74 **Is the presidency imperial or imperilled?**

Imperial	Imperilled
■ Term first used to criticise President Nixon in the 1970s, after he did not consult Congress before military action ■ An imperial presidency would be unconstitutional as the Founding Fathers intended the president's power to be limited ■ President George W. Bush increased presidential power in response to the 9/11 terrorist attacks on America, including detaining terrorist suspects without trial at Guantanamo Bay ■ Obama did not seek congressional approval for his 2011 military intervention in Libya ■ Trump has used executive orders widely, promoted family members, and even claimed he had 'an absolute right' to pardon himself of a crime in 2018	■ Nixon's successor, Gerald Ford, argued the presidency was imperilled by an overly powerful Congress and a large federal bureaucracy ■ Gridlock on presidential Bills, government shutdowns, and overdependence on executive orders and executive agreements can all be seen as signs of an imperilled presidency ■ Obama's weakness was clear when the Senate refused to consider his nominee for the Supreme Court in 2017 ■ Trump's dispute with Congress over funding for his border wall resulted in a 35-day government shutdown, the longest in US history

Exam tip

Make it clear that the use of executive orders and agreements are often a sign of presidential weakness, even though they may appear to be evidence of a president acting in an imperial way. Presidents who are unable to command the support of Congress are forced to use direct authority as a lesser alternative to legislation, but can be easily overruled by the next president.

UK/US comparison

Table 75 **UK/US executives compared**

UK	US
Prime minister is head of government only	President is head of state and head of government
Powers are held by convention	Powers are defined in the Constitution
Prime minister has only one vote in the Cabinet	The president is all powerful in the executive
Cabinet is an important advisory body	Cabinet is not an important source of advice
Cabinet is appointed by the prime minister	Cabinet is nominated by the president and confirmed by the Senate
Members of the Cabinet must also be members of the legislative branch	Members of the Cabinet cannot be members of the legislative branch
Role of Cabinet has been undermined by the growth of the Downing Street machine	Role of Cabinet has been undermined by the growth of EXOP

Do you know?

1 What are the actual and implied powers of the president?

2 What is the role and effectiveness of the Cabinet?

3 What is the role and importance of EXOP?

4 How does presidential power vary depending on circumstances?

5 What are the limits placed on the president?

3.4 The judicial branch

You need to know

- what the Supreme Court is
- how Supreme Court judges are selected and appointed
- the current composition of the Court
- what judicial review is
- why there are debates about the political significance of the Court
- two examples of landmark rulings
- how the judiciary has shaped one area of public policy

Overview: the Supreme Court

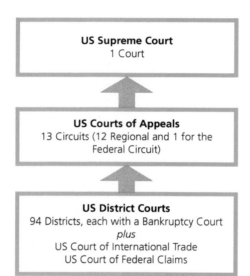

Figure 19 **The structure of the federal courts**

The Supreme Court is an appellate court, meaning it only hears cases appealed from lower courts and it only deals with constitutional matters. It is composed of nine members.

The Supreme Court is independent of the other two branches of government:

- Justices have security of tenure.
- Congress is constitutionally prohibited from reducing the justices' salaries.
- The Supreme Court chooses which cases to hear.
- It is physically separate from the other branches.
- Justices cannot be members of the executive or legislative branches.

Key term

Tenure Employment or time in office.

However, independence of the Supreme Court has been challenged in recent years because:

■ Candidates are appointed and confirmed based on political agendas.
■ There has been executive criticism of Court decisions.
■ The Court is being used by pressure groups to change laws.
■ The Court has become increasingly involved in political debates.
■ *Bush* vs *Gore* (2000) directly involved the Court in the political process.
■ Many justices have worked in the political sphere or have clear connections to political parties

The appointment process

A vacancy must occur
A short list is drawn up based on advice from the Senate Judiciary Committee, White House Staff, the Justice Department and interest groups
Short-listed candidates are given FBI background checks
Candidates are interviewed by the president
Public announcement
Rating given by the ABA Standing Committee on the Federal Judiciary
Hearings are held by the Senate Judiciary Committee
The Senate Judiciary Committee votes on whether to recommend further action
Senate debates
A floor vote in the Senate

Figure 20 **The process for appointing justices**

Table 76 **Strengths and weaknesses of the nomination process**

Strengths	Weaknesses
■ Opportunity to scrutinise candidates ■ Weak candidates can be pushed out before confirmation ■ Candidates must cope with high-pressure scrutiny ■ Creates a degree of unanimity in confirmations ■ Candidates have opportunities to express their thoughts and opinions	■ Politicisation by the president ■ Politicisation by the Senate ■ Politicisation by pressure groups ■ Politicisation by the media ■ Politicisation along partisan lines

The nomination process has become more politicised because of the growing importance of the Supreme Court. This is due to:

- the power of judicial review
- the increasing role of the Court
- the fact that justices have life tenure
- the fact that appointments occur infrequently

Table 77 Current Supreme Court members with year of appointment

Conservative	Liberal
Chief Justice John Roberts (2005)	Ruth Bader-Ginsburg (1993)
Samuel Alito (2006)	Stephen Breyer (1994)
Clarence Thomas (1991)	Sonia Sotomayor (2009)
Neil Gorsuch (2017)	Elena Kagan (2010)
Brett Kavanaugh (2018)	

Synoptic link

UK Supreme Court judges are appointed by an independent body, unlike US justices who are nominated by the president in a highly political process.

The constitutional role of the Supreme Court

The Court's constitutional role is to:

- act as guardian of the Constitution
- interpret the Constitution
- protect citizens' rights

Justices have different views about how they should interpret the Constitution:

Living constitution vs originalism

The living constitution theory believes that:

- The Constitution is open to interpretation through a loose constructionist interpretation.
- The framers kept it vague to allow it to evolve as the USA changed.
- The role of the Supreme Court is to modernise the Constitution.

Originalists believe that:

- Like all laws, the Constitution is a dead document, not open to new interpretation, so a strict constructionist approach applies.
- Interpretations should be based on the original intention of the framers.
- The role of the Supreme Court is to apply the standard of 1788 to modern America.

Key terms

Living constitution A theory that the US Constitution is living and therefore open to new interpretations.

Originalism A theory that the Constitution should only be considered by the original intentions of the framers.

Strict/loose constructionist Strict constructionists stick closely to the words of the Constitution, while loose constructionists give greater interpretation to what is written, going beyond the words of the text.

Judicial review

The Supreme Court's main power is that of judicial review. By this power, the Court can:

- interpret the meaning of the Constitution
- strike down government actions
- strike down legislation
- strike down state laws and actions
- effectively amend the Constitution

The power of judicial review is controversial because:

- It is not expressly stated in the Constitution.
- The Supreme Court granted itself this power in the cases of *Marbury* vs *Madison*, 1803 (federal law) and *Fletcher* vs *Peck*, 1810 (state law).
- It undermines the principle of a separation of powers.
- It gives too much power to unelected and unaccountable judges.
- Some justices, generally liberals, have been criticised for judicial activism.
- Some justices, generally conservatives, prefer to practise judicial restraint.

Key terms

Judicial review The power to review executive and legislative actions and declare them unconstitutional.

Judicial activism Judicial decisions that interpret the Constitution in a new way. For example, in 2015 the Supreme Court ruled that there is a constitutional right to same-sex marriage, something the framers of the Constitution did not intend. Judicial activism is sometimes referred to as 'legislating from the bench'.

Judicial restraint The practice of avoiding overturning legal precedents (previous decisions made by the Court).

Landmark rulings

A landmark ruling is a decision by the Court that establishes a new legal principle. Two examples are *Brown* vs *Board of Education of Topeka* (1954) and *Obergefell* vs *Hodges* (2015), which are outlined in Table 78.

Table 78 **Two examples of landmark rulings**

Ruling	Significance	Controversy and debate
Brown vs *Board of Education of Topeka* (1954)	<ul><li>Court unanimously declared doctrine of 'separate but equal' unconstitutional</li><li>Ended policy of educational segregation</li></ul>	<ul><li>Perceived as an attack on states' rights in the South</li><li>Federal troops needed to implement desegregation in Little Rock, Arkansas (1957)</li></ul>
Obergefell vs *Hodges* (2015)	<ul><li>Ruled same-sex marriage was a fundamental constitutional right</li><li>A victory for loose constructionists</li></ul>	<ul><li>Strict constructionists criticised decision as framers of the Constitution did not intend same-sex marriage to be legal</li><li>Many Christians believed the ruling infringed their religious freedom</li><li>Seen as an imposition by the federal government that undermined states' rights and federalism</li></ul>

The Supreme Court and public policy

The Supreme Court has played a crucial role in determining many areas of US public policy, including abortion.

Table 79 **The impact of the Supreme Court on one area of public policy: abortion**

Public policy	Court decisions	Impact
Abortion	*Roe* vs *Wade*, 1973	Created a right to abortion
	Planned Parenthood vs *Casey*, 1992	'Undue burdens' could not be placed on a woman's right to choose
	Gonzales vs *Carhart*, 2007	Allowed a ban on partial birth abortions
	Whole Woman's Health vs *Hellerstedt*, 2016	Struck down some state-based restrictions

UK/US comparison

Table 80 **Comparison of the UK and US Supreme Courts**

UK	US
12 members	9 members
Nominated by an independent commission and confirmed by the monarch	Nominated by the president and confirmed by the Senate
Small groups of justices hear each case	All justices hear all cases
Tenure until 75	Life tenure
Paid from an independent fund	Paid through Congress, but pay cannot be cut
Cannot overturn primary legislation	Can strike down any legislation or governmental action
Increasingly used in political issues	Increasingly used in political issues
Protects rights through the Human Rights Act (HRA)	Protects rights through the amendments
Cases can be appealed to the European Court of Human Rights or the European Court of Justice (for now)	There is no higher authority

Do you know?

1 How are justices appointed?

2 What are the criticisms of the appointment process?

3 What is the basis of judicial review?

4 How is the current court composed?

5 What are the issues relating to theories of judicial interpretation?

3.5 The electoral process and direct democracy

You need to know

- the electoral systems used in the US
- the features of presidential and congressional campaigns
- how candidates are selected and nominated
- debates about the workings and role of the Electoral College
- factors that win and lose elections
- debates about campaign finance
- how direct democracy works at state level
- the factors that influence voting behaviour
- how split ticketing works
- why US elections have a high level of abstention

Elections and electoral system

The USA uses the first-past-the-post electoral system and is a two-party system.

Elections take place at the following intervals:

- presidential elections: every 4 years
- congressional elections: every 2 years, either during a presidential election or mid-terms are held between presidential elections

The whole of the House of Representatives and a third of the Senate is elected every 2 years. The president is elected via the Electoral College.

Presidential elections

Requirements

To become president, there are four constitutional requirements and many desirable non-constitutional qualities.

Table 81 **Constitutional requirements and non-constitutional qualities for becoming president**

Constitutional	Non-constitutional
■ Be a natural-born citizen ■ Be 35 years old or over ■ Be resident for 14 years ■ Not to have served two previous terms	■ Experience of political office ■ The support of a major party ■ A positive image ■ Financial resources ■ A strong organisational structure ■ The right image for television, radio and social media ■ Relevant policies

The invisible primary

The period between candidates announcing their intention to run and the Iowa caucus is known as the invisible primary.

Candidates campaign to win the invisible primary by becoming the 'front runner' (the person with the most funds and highest poll numbers before the primaries begin). However, winning the invisible primary does not guarantee the nomination.

Primaries and caucuses

In primaries, members of the public are able to elect delegates to a party's national convention. These delegates will select the party's presidential candidate.

The primary process begins with the Iowa caucus, usually in January or February of an election year.

The party national committee determines the order and timings of state-based primary votes, but the rules and means of allocating delegates are left up to the party in each state.

State-based parties can choose to have:
- a primary vote or a caucus
- an open vote (meaning anyone can vote) or closed vote (meaning only registered party supporters can vote)
- winner takes all (the plurality winner gets all the delegates) or proportional (some means of sharing out delegates based on voting outcomes)

Voter turnout in primaries is usually low, but it is determined by factors such as:
- the timing of the primary
- the type of primary
- whether it is a primary or caucus (caucuses are much lower because of the time commitments)
- who turns out (usually older, white and high income/education)
- the competitiveness of the contest
- whether or not the outcome has been decided

Key terms

Iowa caucus The Republican and Democrat party caucuses in Iowa always mark the start of the presidential primary race.

Invisible primary The period before the official primary campaign begins.

Primaries Elections by state to determine delegate support for a presidential candidate.

Caucuses A series of meetings to determine delegates for a presidential candidate.

Exam tip

A strong performance in the invisible primary will not win the nomination, but a bad performance can end a candidacy.

Table 82 **Positives and negatives of the primary process**

Positive	Negative
■ Weakens the power of party bosses ■ More opportunity to participate ■ Greater scrutiny of candidates ■ Time to assess the candidates ■ Greater voter choice ■ Candidates present themselves to the public ■ People get to know the candidates	■ Forces poor candidates on parties ■ Low turnout ■ Apathy from the electorate ■ Lengthens the electoral process ■ 'Crazy' candidates ■ Expensive process ■ Campaigns can become personal battles and populist

National nominating conventions

Formal functions

National nominating conventions have three formal functions:

1 choosing a presidential candidate
2 choosing a vice presidential candidate
3 deciding the party platform

However, these functions are no longer very important because:

■ candidates are chosen through the primaries
■ presidential candidates now pick their vice-presidential running-mates
■ presidential candidates choose their own platform

Informal functions

The informal functions of conventions have become increasingly important for election campaigns. These functions include:

■ unifying the party after the primary campaigns
■ enthusing the party base to campaign for the nominee
■ winning over voters
■ generating positive media reporting and a bounce in the opinion polls

The Electoral College

The Electoral College is a shadow congress with one job: to elect the president.

Electoral College votes are allocated based on:

■ the number of seats a state has in the House of Representatives
■ the number of senators a state has
■ three Electoral College votes are awarded to Washington DC

There are 538 Electoral College votes in total and a successful candidate needs a clear majority to win: 270.

> ### Key terms
>
> **National nominating conventions** Meetings of party delegates held every 4 years to choose a presidential candidate for the party.
>
> **Electoral College** The body that elects the president.

> ### Synoptic link
>
> The Electoral College is set out in the Constitution, so any reform would require a constitutional amendment.

How the Electoral College works

- Voters elect delegates from their states, who have the job of choosing the president on their behalf.
- Nowadays many delegates are bound, meaning they have to vote the way the state has voted, but some could become rogue electors and vote for someone else.
- Most states award all their Electoral College votes on a winner takes all basis, meaning a narrow win in a swing state can give a candidate all their delegates. For this reason, candidates can win the Electoral College without winning a majority of the popular vote.
- In Maine and Nebraska Electoral College votes are allocated by congressional district, with the state-wide winner of the popular vote gaining the two 'senate' votes.

Table 83 **Positives and negatives of the Electoral College**

Positives	Negatives
■ It promotes federalism ■ It promotes a clear two-horse race ■ It enhances a presidential mandate ■ It ensures national support for a candidate ■ It usually works	■ Large states are underrepresented ■ It discriminates against third parties ■ It distorts the results ■ It is determined by a few swing states ■ 2000 and 2016 saw winners who lost the popular vote

Possible reforms

Proposed reforms include:

- a national popular vote, but small states oppose this
- congressional district system, but gerrymandering means the wrong result is more likely
- a proportional system, but this would make a majority much harder to achieve
- getting rid of individual electors, but this would require a constitutional amendment

Factors affecting presidential elections

The winner of a presidential election is often determined by:

- the campaigns
- the incumbency factor
- media
- campaign finance
- issues
- leadership

Key terms

Rogue elector An elector who does not vote for the candidate his/her state chose.

Swing states States that could choose a candidate from either party.

Gerrymandering The practice of redrawing electoral district boundaries in order to give a political advantage to one group.

Campaign finance Money spent fighting an election.

Campaigns

What campaigns need to do to be successful:
- enthuse the public to participate
- have an effective 'Get out the vote' strategy
- have a positive media presence
- target events and promotions in swing states
- raise sufficient funds
- perform well in debates

Incumbency

Primaries

- Incumbent presidents rarely face a serious primary challenge.
- They can focus on fundraising and preparing for the election campaign, while their rival is being attacked by their own party.

Election campaigns

- Presidents have a record of achievement to be judged by.
- Presidents have had the opportunity to use federal pork to win support in key states.
- Presidents gain higher media attention.
- If a crisis occurs, it gives the incumbent the chance to appear presidential by dealing with it effectively.

Media

How a candidate is portrayed by the media is crucial to success. Media can be either:
- earned, meaning press coverage that costs the candidate nothing
- bought, meaning paid for by the campaign, like adverts

Since the 1950s, television has dominated the debate, with political shows, presidential debates and adverts displaying a candidate's ideas and attacking opponents.

In the twenty-first century social media has played an increasingly important role, with websites and viral videos promoting candidates and social media platforms like Twitter and Facebook allowing candidates to contact voters directly, generate earned media and shape the debate.

Campaign finance

Money is seen as essential in US elections because it funds:

- advertising
- staff and campaign teams
- travel
- support staff
- holding events
- polling

Attempts to regulate the amount of money being spent include:

- the Federal Election Campaign Act, 1974
- the creation of the Federal Election Commission to regulate elections, 1974
- the Bipartisan Campaign Finance Reform Act, 2002

These regulations were limited by Supreme Court rulings, which have protected political donations as a form of freedom of speech.

The most important Supreme Court decision was *Citizens United* vs *FEC Election Commission* in 2010:

- The Court ruled that the 1st Amendment gave pressure groups, unions and corporations the same rights to free speech as individuals.
- This means that while the amount of money an official campaign or a PAC can raise (hard money) can be regulated, the amount of money a private organisation spends campaigning cannot.
- This led to the creation of super PACs to raise soft money.

Impact of money

- The cost of elections has increased dramatically since 2000.
- However, candidates and super PACs are usually well matched, so money was only a significant determining factor in 2008 when Barack Obama raised more than double the amount of his rival John McCain.
- In 2016 Donald Trump was elected despite being outspent by Hillary Clinton (Trump spent $398 million compared to Clinton's $768 million).

Key terms

PAC A political committee that supports candidates with hard money. There are limits on how much they can raise and donate.

Hard money Money raised directly for a candidate's official campaign. Hard money is regulated.

Super PAC A political committee that raises soft money for election campaigns. There are no limits on how much money they can raise and donate.

Soft money Money that is not directly linked to candidates' campaigns, although it may support their election. Soft money is unregulated.

Direct democracy

The USA has direct democracy at state level only, so the degree to which it is used varies across the country.

Table 84 **Direct democracy at state level in the US**

Type of direct Democracy	Detail
Referendums	State legislature suggests a new law and asks the public to vote on it in a referendum
Initiatives/citizens' propositions	The public initiates a vote on a new proposal. A set number of signatures must be collected, and the measure is then put on the ballot to be voted on by the electorate. Allows popular legislation to spread between states, e.g. legalisation of marijuana
Recall elections	Public can trigger a 'recall election' for an elected official if they can collect enough signatures. If the official then loses the recall election he/she will be removed from office. Rarely used as requires large numbers of signatures

Voting behaviour

Core voting coalitions

American parties are umbrella organisations that cover many different groups. This makes the national party a coalition of different groups, which may have similar or very different views on some issues.

Table 85 **Typical party support among groups**

Groups that tend to support Democrats	Groups that tend to support Republicans
Women	Men
Younger voters	Older voters
Racial minorities	White
Urban residents	Rural
Higher education (postgraduate)	Lower education (high school only)
Northeast and west coast	Central and southern USA
Low religious attendance	High religious attendance

Why groups vote as they do

Race

- Democrat support for civil rights legislation and action since the 1960s
- Democrat support for affirmative action programs
- high levels of poverty in minority groups increase support for Democrat welfare programs
- Democrats have a higher degree of black representation
- Democrat support for immigration reform
- Republican opposition to affirmative action and civil rights legislation
- Republican threats to 'build a wall' and deport illegal immigrants

Religion

- Republican opposition to abortion
- appeals to the religious right by Reagan and George W. Bush
- Democrat support for socially liberal policies that conflict with religious teachings

Gender

- Republican opposition to the Equal Rights Amendment
- Democrat support/Republican opposition to abortion
- Democrat promotion of social welfare programs
- Republican focus on military and conflict

Education

- the lower educated tend to be lower earners and want Republican job protection
- the lower educated tend to favour Republican pledges to curb immigration to protect jobs
- higher education has a liberalising effect

Other factors in voting behaviour

Voters are also influenced by:

- issues raised during the campaign
- candidates' personalities, leadership, expertise

Realigning elections

Realigning elections represent an important turning point in long-term voting behaviour. Examples include:

- **1932**: shift from Republicans to Democrats in support of F.D. Roosevelt's 'New Deal'.
- **1968**: shift from Democrats to Republicans, with Richard Nixon taking the presidency. Nixon went on to adopt a 'Southern Strategy' in which Republicans appealed to southern voters who had previously supported the Democrats but disliked the civil rights movement. The South had long been a Democrat heartland, but the 1964, 1968 and 1972 elections ended this tradition, making it easier for Republicans to win nationally.
- **1992:** shift from Republicans to Democrats, with the election of President Bill Clinton. California changed from being a Republican state to the Democrat state that it is today, as did a number of northeastern states.

Key term

Religious right People who support a conservative religious-based ideology.

Exam tip

Remember that while most Republicans oppose abortion, there are exceptions. Two Republican senators, Susan Collins and Lisa Murkowski, are seen as relatively pro-choice. There are also members of the Democratic party who are either pro-life or socially conservative on other issues.

Exam tip

Voting by groups refers to general trends and there will be many exceptions within each group. Coalitions of groups can also cause factions by having contradictory aims.

Split-ticket voting

Split-ticket voting is:

- when a voter is voting for multiple posts in the same election, and chooses to vote for candidates of more than one party
- less common in recent years as politics has become more polarised

Abstention

Turnout (abstention) in US elections is generally low, e.g. 55.7% in 2016 presidential election. This can be explained by the following factors:

- too-frequent elections
- FPTP electoral system — lack of choice and wasted votes
- voter registration requirements
- felony disenfranchisement
- disillusionment with politicians
- negative campaigning
- lack of competitive districts due to gerrymandering

UK/US comparison

Table 86 **A comparison of UK/US elections**

UK	US
Elections are every 5 years, but can be earlier	Congressional elections are every 2 years; presidential elections are every 4 years, without fail
Election campaigns are usually 4–6 weeks	Election campaigns can last up to 2 years
Party leader is chosen by their party	Candidates are chosen by the public
Need majority support in the House of Commons	Need a majority in the Electoral College
Television advertising is banned	Advertising is unrestricted
Cost around £80 million in total	Cost over $2 billion just for the presidency
There are leadership debates	There are presidential debates

Do you know?

1 How are the presidential candidates chosen?

2 How does the primary system work?

3 What is the importance of the party conventions?

4 Why are US elections so expensive, and why have attempts to regulate them failed?

5 What are the strengths and weaknesses of the Electoral College?

3.6 US political parties

You need to know

- how the main parties are structured
- the core principles and policies of the Democrats and Republicans
- the main factions and divisions within the parties
- which groups support which party and why

Party policies

Party structure

The main parties have a federal structure:

- **National committees:** oversee the primary process, national policies and fundraising.
- **Congressional leadership:** congressional leaders will develop policy and coordinate campaigns.
- **State parties:** each state has its own version of the national party where candidate selection, delegate selection and local policies are carried out.

Democrats

The Democrats tend to:

- hold progressive attitudes on social policy
- favour greater government intervention
- promote social welfare policies

Republicans

Republicans tend to:

- hold conservative attitudes on social policy
- favour limited government intervention
- protect American economic interests
- promote individual responsibility in welfare

Synoptic link

US party organisation is much weaker and less centralised than in the UK. State parties are important, and there are no official national party leaders.

Synoptic link

The different policies of the two parties help to explain the composition of their core voting coalitions, as each party's platform tends to appeal to different groups.

Table 87 **2016 party policies**

Democrats	Republicans
Women should have the right to choose an abortion	A foetus has the right to life
Support for same-sex marriage	Promotion of marriage between a man and a woman
Reduce the impact of crime in minorities	Support mandatory prison sentences
Support for environmental measures	Support fracking and the use of fossil fuels
National minimum wage should be increased	Minimum wage rates should be set at the state level
Make wealthy people and large corporations pay their fair share of taxes	Reduce corporate taxes
Support the Affordable Care Act	Repeal the Affordable Care Act

Internal party divisions

> **Key term**
>
> **Factions** Groups that have different opinions within a party.

Table 88 **Democrat** factions

Policy	Moderate Democrats	Liberal Democrats
Trade	Free trade, support Trans-Pacific Partnership	Greater regulation of Wall Street
Education	Support for disadvantaged students	Free college education
Healthcare	Public private partnership in Affordable Care Act	Healthcare provision for all
Military	Strong military and global role	Military cuts and limited intervention
Guns	Limited gun restrictions	Strong gun restrictions
Immigration	Immigration reform	Pathway to citizenship

Table 89 **Republican factions**

Policy	Moderate Republicans	Social Conservatives	Fiscal Conservatives
Trade	Prioritise small businesses	Protectionism	Total free trade
Spending	Balanced budgets	Increases to military, defence and desirable social programs	Severe cuts to all areas
Welfare	Government safety net with individual responsibility	Individual responsibility	Reduce/eliminate federal welfare
Military	Support a strong military	Strong military and American intervention	Oppose military intervention
Immigration	Support for controlled immigration	Opposed to immigration	Favour immigration for jobs/oppose spending on immigration controls
Minimum wage	Reduce	Reduce	Abolish
Abortion	Opposed, except in some circumstances	Opposed in all circumstances	No strong position

Third parties and independents

The USA has a two-party system. Third party or independent members of Congress:

- are rare (only two independent senators were elected to the 116th Congress, from a total of 535 representatives and senators)
- can influence the outcome of close elections, e.g. Ralph Nader (Green Party) took 2.7% of the vote in the 2000 presidential election, and probably prevented Democrat Al Gore from winning
- may influence the policies of the main parties

Party decline or renewal?

Table 90 **Are US parties in a state of decline or renewal?**

Decline	Renewal
- Weak control of parties by leaders in Congress and presidents - Primaries reduce influence of party leadership in candidate selection - Party platforms (agreed party policies) often ignored by presidents	- Increasing number of party unity votes in Congress - Decline in split-ticket voting - US remains a two-party system - Rise of hyperpartisanship means public are more deeply divided along party lines

UK/US comparison

Table 91 **Comparison of UK and US party politics**

UK	US
Strong party control	Weak party
Two-party with multi-party elements	Two-party domination
Strong party unity	Weak party unity
Ideological cohesion	Coalition of factions
Limits on campaign activity	Almost no limits on campaign activity
Core role in contesting elections	Role undermined by candidates and super PACs
Centralised structure	Federal structure

Synoptic links

- The number of moderate Republicans and moderate Democrats in Congress has fallen as the parties have become more polarised. This means that bipartisanship is less common, making gridlock more likely.

- The National Rifle Association (NRA) pressure group is a major donor to the Republican Party. Unions donate heavily to the Democrats. This could suggest the parties are not in decline.

Key term

Party unity vote Vote in which the majority of Democrats vote differently from the majority of Republicans.

Exam tip

You need to be able to explain why US parties are relatively weak. Consider their federalised structure and the lack of a powerful party leader within Congress.

Do you know?

1 How are the main parties structured?
2 What are the core principles and policies of the Democrats and Republicans?
3 What are the internal factions and divisions within each party?
4 Which groups support which party?
5 Why do key groups support a party?

3.7 US pressure groups

You need to know
- the different types of pressure groups in American politics
- what methods pressure groups use to influence decision makers
- how pressure groups fund elections
- the debate concerning the power of US pressure groups

Political pluralism

Pressure groups contribute to political pluralism in the USA by providing:
- broader representation than political parties
- social and activist campaigns for people to participate in, via interest groups or promotional groups
- agenda building, as high-profile pressure groups can set the political agenda
- public education, researching and publishing reports to support their positions
- pressure on legislatures, as pressure groups will publicise voting records to ensure representatives vote as members wish

Influencing decision making

Pressure groups find it easier to influence decision making if they have:
- a strong and activist membership
- financial resources
- policy expertise, particularly interest groups
- a role in a specific sector, usually by professional groups
- legal expertise
- support across a range of states and districts

Methods and tactics

American pressure groups use a number of methods and tactics to achieve their goals as outlined in Table 92.

Key terms

Political pluralism The participation in politics of many different groups from across the whole of society.

Interest groups Groups that campaign for their own interests, e.g. unions, the National Rifle Association (NRA).

Promotional groups Groups that campaign for a cause on behalf of others, e.g. the American Civil Liberties Union (ACLU).

Exam tip

If analysing political pluralism in the US, remember that elitist theory argues that politics is dominated by a powerful elite, and that this extends to pressure groups as well. Elite theorists would argue that wealthy and well-connected pressure groups have far more influence than others.

Table 92 **Methods and tactics used by US pressure groups**

Electioneering	■ Pressure groups can spend vast sums campaigning on behalf of a favoured candidate
Endorsement	■ The public backing of a powerful group can help build support for a candidate
Lobbying	■ Meeting with members of Congress or the executive to persuade them to follow a particular course or vote a particular way ■ May use professional lobbyists, or mobilise members to lobby their representatives ■ Professional lobbying firms often employ former members of the legislature or the executive as lobbyists (the 'revolving-door syndrome')
Advising	■ Meeting with members of Congress and giving them advice on how to vote and summarising Bills on their behalf ■ May appear in front of Congressional committees ■ May assist executive in implementation of policies ■ Provide *amicus curiae* briefs to the Supreme Court
Test cases	■ Pressure groups may use the legal system to achieve their goals through bringing a case to the Supreme Court
Organising activities	■ Protests and rallies ■ Persuading members of the public to contact representatives

> **Key term**
>
> *Amicus curiae* **briefs**
> Friend of the court briefs provide advice and information to justices that may help them in understanding a case.

> **Synoptic link**
>
> The right to lobby is protected in the Constitution in the 1st Amendment under 'right to petition the government'.

Table 93 **The National Rifle Association (NRA) case study**

Influence	Methods	Power
The NRA has prevented politicians from tightening gun regulations	■ Legal challenges ■ Lobbying ■ Organising an activist membership to lobby ■ Campaign funding	■ Most Americans favour the right to bear arms, so there are no strong countervailing forces to the NRA ■ The NRA is able to prevent debate and discussion in Congress on even minor gun regulation, despite regular mass shootings

Pressure group funding of elections

Pressure groups play an important role in electoral finance:

■ They choose to support candidates who agree with their objectives, e.g. pro-life groups usually back Republican candidates.

■ Incumbents receive most funding from pressure groups. This gives Washington insiders a big advantage over candidates who have not held office before.

■ Pressure group funding reinforces incumbency, meaning that incumbents are more likely to be elected than other candidates.

■ Pressure group funding of candidates contributes to the existence of iron triangles.

> **Key terms**
>
> Electoral finance The ways in which election campaigns are funded.
>
> Iron triangle A strong relationship between Congress, the government, and a specific set of pressure groups, e.g. pharmaceutical companies, oil companies. Decisions are taken to benefit all three, but the interests of the rest of society may be neglected.

- PACs and super PACS are the main way that pressure groups donate to election campaigns.
- Super PACs have led to greater amounts of money being spent in US elections: an estimated $6.5 billion was spent in the presidential and congressional elections in 2016.

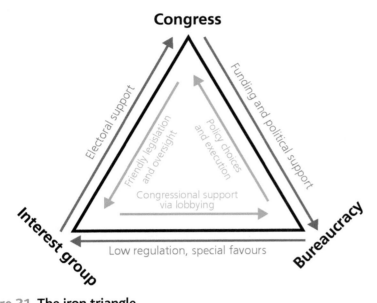

Figure 21 **The iron triangle**

Power of pressure groups

Table 94 **Are US pressure groups too powerful?**

No	Yes
They provide information and assistance to promote better-quality legislation and government action	Information and assistance is in the interest groups' vested interest, not the national interest
They provide public education on key issues	They can manipulate the public on important issues
They provide more effective representation than the parties	They act in their own interest and are not accountable or well regulated
Lobbyists have to follow some regulations	Lobbyists may have unfair access, particularly because of the revolving-door syndrome
They defend constitutional rights and are themselves crucial to 1st Amendment freedom of speech and association	They can prevent desirable constitutional change from being achieved, e.g. the NRA and gun control
They scrutinise the work of elected officials	They manipulate and hold power over elected officials
They create opportunities for participation which is important in a pluralist society	Participation in political parties may be reduced if people join pressure groups instead
Members of Congress are accountable to their voters, not pressure groups	Wealthy pressure groups and donors have too much influence. This is elitist
Candidates who raise the most money do not always win elections, e.g. Clinton raised more than Trump in 2016	Super PACs may undermine the role of parties by encouraging candidates to vote in accordance with super PAC wishes rather than party policy

UK/US comparison

Table 95 Comparison of UK/US pressure groups

UK	US
Limited electioneering role	Strong electioneering role
Strong union presence	Weak union presence
Limitations on donations and spending	Very few limits on donations and spending
Difficulty of lobbying	Lobbying culture
Focus on the executive	All branches of government effective targets
Limited constitutional protection	Protection under the 1st Amendment
Usually weaker than political parties	Often stronger than political parties

Do you know?

1 How do pressure groups contribute to political pluralism?
2 What different methods do pressure groups use?
3 What is a super PAC?
4 What is an iron triangle?

3.8 Civil rights

Protection of civil rights and liberties

Civil rights and civil liberties are protected in the USA in the following ways:

Key terms

Civil rights Additional government protections to prevent groups of citizens from being discriminated against, e.g. the 1965 Voting Rights Act prevented discrimination against African–Americans.

Civil liberties Freedoms enjoyed by all Americans, e.g. the right to freedom of speech.

Table 96 How civil rights and liberties are protected in the USA

Method	Protection
The Constitution (1787)	■ Protects citizens from an overly powerful government ■ Checks and balances limit the powers of each branch of government ■ Article III established the US Supreme Court, a court of final appeal if citizens feel their rights have been infringed
The Bill of Rights (1791)	This protects civil liberties of US citizens from the government, e.g.: ■ 1st Amendment (freedom of religion, speech, press and assembly) ■ 2nd Amendment (the right to keep and bear arms) ■ 6th Amendment (the right to a fair trial) ■ 8th Amendment (prohibits cruel and unusual punishments)
Subsequent amendments to the Constitution	■ 13th Amendment (1865) abolished slavery ■ 14th Amendment (1868) gave former slaves full citizenship, 'equal protection' under the law, a right to 'due process' ■ 19th Amendment (1920) gave women the vote ■ 24th amendment (1964) banned taxes on voting
Landmark rulings of the Supreme Court	The Court applies the Constitution to modern civil rights issues: ■ *Brown* vs *Topeka Board of Education* (1954) struck down the doctrine of 'separate but equal' that had underpinned segregation in America's South ■ *Roe* vs *Wade* (1973) ruled that women had the right to an abortion in the early stages of pregnancy ■ *Obergefell* vs *Hodges* (2015) gave same-sex couples the right to marry

The role of pressure groups

Pressure groups play an important role in supporting rights:

- The right of citizens to form pressure groups is itself a civil liberty, part of the rights of free speech and assembly defined in the 1st Amendment.
- Pressure groups have led many campaigns to support rights.
- Liberal groups defend the rights of African–Americans, women, and the LGBT community.
- Conservative groups defend religious rights, the rights of the unborn child, and gun rights.
- Social movements are increasingly important, e.g. Black Lives Matter, the Women's March, #MeToo.

Table 97 **Examples of pressure groups campaigning for rights**

Group	Campaign focus
National Association for the Advancement of Colored People (NAACP)	Civil rights for African–Americans
American Civil Liberties Union	Civil liberties of all individuals
National Organisation for Women (NOW)	Women's rights
GLAAD	LGBTQ rights
Planned Parenthood	Abortion rights
Family Research Council	Rights of the unborn child (anti-abortion), religious freedom
National Rifle Association (NRA)	Right to bear arms

Case study: the impact of civil rights on US politics — race

The civil rights movement

The civil rights movement:

- used a range of different campaign methods, including direct action
- exposed the violence and racism experienced by African–Americans
- resulted in a landmark Supreme Court case, *Brown* vs *Topeka*
- led to Congress passing the Civil Rights Acts of 1957, 1964, and 1968, and the 1965 Voting Rights Act
- was successful in passing the 24th Amendment

> ### Key term
>
> Civil rights movement
> The campaign for equal rights for African–Americans, at its height in the 1950s and 1960s.

Voting rights

Protection

Congress has passed laws to protect voting rights:

- the Voting Rights Act, 1965
- the Voting Rights Act Reauthorization, 2006

These Acts required areas with diverse populations and records of segregation to get approval from the Attorney General before making any changes to voting laws.

Attacks

- In *Shelby County* v. *Holder*, 2013, the Court struck down a key provision of the Voting Rights Act. As a result, nine states had introduced photo ID requirements by 2016.
- Voting rights are also restricted by felony disenfranchisement, with some states banning anyone with a criminal conviction from ever voting again.
- Voter ID laws and felony disenfranchisement do not specifically restrict the right of minorities to vote, but they disproportionately impact on minority individuals who are less likely to hold or afford a valid ID and are much more likely have been convicted.

Affirmative action

The main areas of affirmative action have been:

- busing (ruled unconstitutional)
- quotas (ruled unconstitutional)
- preferential consideration in college admissions
- preferential consideration in school admissions
- preferential consideration in employment and promotion
- affirmative racial gerrymandering to produce majority-minority districts

> ### Key term
>
> **Felony disenfranchisement**
> Denying a person the right to vote based on criminal convictions.

> ### Synoptic link
>
> The arguments for and against allowing prisoners the right to vote are similar in the UK and USA, but there is a far greater racial dynamic in the USA.

> ### Key terms
>
> **Affirmative action** A program giving beneficial treatment to minority groups (usually African–American). This 'positive discrimination' aims to reverse the inequalities faced by African–Americans, and to try to make up for past injustice.
>
> **Affirmative racial gerrymandering** The practice of redrawing electoral district boundaries to create majority-minority districts in order to benefit minorities.
>
> **Majority-minority district** Electoral district that contains a majority of voters from an ethnic minority. This makes it more likely that a representative from an ethnic minority will be chosen for that district.

Affirmative action has been a divisive issue in US politics:

- Liberals thought it was fair as it took account of existing inequality.
- Conservatives argued it was a form of reverse discrimination.
- Most Republicans are highly critical of affirmative action, most Democrats support it.
- The Supreme Court has also been divided on the issue, but in *Fisher* vs *University of Texas* (2016) it ruled that affirmative action was legal, provided that certain criteria were met.

Black Lives Matter

- #BlackLivesMatter began trending on Twitter in 2013 after George Zimmerman was acquitted for shooting dead unarmed teenager Trayvon Martin.
- Subsequent police shootings of unarmed African–Americans resulted in street protests and riots, e.g. the Ferguson unrest, 2014.
- The movement highlights the racial bias within US society and police brutality towards unarmed African–Americans.

The rise of the Alt-Right

- The rise of the Alt-Right poses a new threat to civil rights.
- President Trump's association with some leading Alt-Right figures led to fears that the gains of the civil rights movement could be at risk.
- Murders and mass shootings by far-right extremists and white supremacists have risen significantly since 2014.

UK/US comparison

Table 98 **UK/US comparison of rights protections**

UK	US
Rights are mostly protected through the Supreme Court	Rights are often protected by the Supreme Court
Parliament and the prime minister also play meaningful roles in rights protection	Congress and the executive can play a meaningful role in rights protection
Rights are defined by common law and the Human Rights Act	Rights are set out in the Constitution, mostly in the amendments
Rights are not entrenched	Rights are entrenched
The Supreme Court has no power to strike down statute law or executive actions that breach the Human Rights Act	The Supreme Court can strike down any law or action that breaches a constitutional right
The Supreme Court has no power of enforcement	The Supreme Court has no power of enforcement
Rights protection has been growing since 2000	Rights protections have been growing since the 1950s

Do you know?

1 Give examples of cases dealing with civil rights.
2 How have voting rights been upheld and infringed?
3 What are the arguments surrounding affirmative action?
4 How have pressure groups supported rights?

End of section 3 questions

1 What are the main principles of the US Constitution?
2 What is federalism?
3 How effective is the Supreme Court at checking the other branches of government?
4 Why has the appointment of Supreme Court justices been criticised?
5 What powers are held by Congress?
6 Why is the Senate seen as more prestigious than the House?
7 How effective is Congress at checking the other branches of government?
8 What are the differences between EXOP and the Cabinet?
9 What is affirmative action and why has it been criticised?
10 Why is the electoral process so long in US politics?
11 What are the arguments for reforming the Electoral College?
12 Which groups of voters support the Democrats and why?
13 Which groups of voters support the Republicans and why?
14 How significant are pressure groups in US politics?
15 To what extent do pressure groups undermine democracy?

4 Political ideas

4.1 Liberalism

You need to know
- the core ideas of liberalism
- the difference between classical and modern liberalism
- the debates within liberalism
- the key ideas of:
  - ☐ Locke
  - ☐ Wollstonecraft
  - ☐ Mill
  - ☐ Rawls
  - ☐ Green
  - ☐ Friedan
- how these thinkers' ideas relate to human nature, the state, society and the economy

Liberalism developed over the seventeenth and eighteenth centuries and was:
- a reaction against the divine rights of the king, religious obedience and hierarchies of medieval societies
- based on science, reason and philosophy

Core ideas

Table 99 **Core ideas of liberalism**

Idea	Meaning	Related concepts
Individualism	■ Individuals are supreme ■ A positive view of human nature ■ Self-interest is a prime motivator	Egotistical individualism: individuals act to further their own interests
Rationalism	■ Individuals apply logic and reason and do what makes rational sense ■ Individuals act in their own, rational, self-interest but also what is rationally in the best interests of society	Individualism
Liberty	■ Society is strongest when individuals are free to pursue their own goals without regulation or restrictions	Economic liberalism
State	■ Government rules with the consent of the governed, through a social contract ■ Mankind is capable of creating a state ■ The state should be limited by having a constitution and individual rights ■ State power and institutions should be separated ■ Tolerance of individualism and diversity	■ Social contract ■ Limited government ■ Rights protection ■ Separation of powers ■ Mechanistic theory: humans are capable of creating a state to meet their needs
Equality	■ Individuals are born equal ■ Equality exists under the rule of law ■ There should be equality of opportunity for everyone ■ Different views and behaviours are to be tolerated as individual choices	■ Social justice ■ Foundational equality ■ Toleration ■ Formal equality

Idea	Meaning	Related concepts
Liberal democracy	■ Promotion of a limited government with rights protections ■ Government rules by the will of the people, through elections, referendums and so on, but the government is able to ensure society is free ■ Society is based on a meritocracy	■ Civil rights ■ Civil liberties ■ Democracy

Types of liberalism

Classical liberalism

Classical liberalism believes in:

■ **Revolutionary potential:** if/when a government or institutions become too powerful and infringe on individual liberties, the people are entitled to rise up in revolution and overthrow the government, but private property must be respected.

■ **Negative liberty:** everything is legal until it is prohibited, meaning a person is free to do as they please until it is expressly banned or restricted. The fewer restrictions, the great the liberty.

■ **Minimal state:** while a state is necessary, it should do little and only when required, such as legislating and taxing.

■ **Laissez-faire capitalism:** economic measures should be left to market forces without interference or restrictions from the state, such as duties, tariffs, taxes and regulations. Private property must be protected.

Key thinkers include:
■ John Locke
■ Mary Wollstonecraft
■ John Stuart Mill

Modern liberalism

Modern liberalism believes in:

■ **Positive liberty:** market forces and social conditions limit individual freedoms, so individual liberty needs to be clearly protected by introducing laws. This would allow social justice and equality to be achieved.

■ **Enlarged state:** in order to protect individuals from socioeconomic threats, it is the role of the state to act through collective measures and enlarging the role of the state through taxation, regulation and legislation.

■ **Constitutional reform:** to enable the enlargement of the state, constitutional reform is necessary to ensure the state remains democratic, representative and limited, whilst also carrying out more functions.

Key terms

Economic liberalism The idea that the economy should be free from government interference.

Social contract The government rules by the consent of the people and if it breaks this agreement it can be replaced.

Limited government State institutions are restricted in power by constitutional laws and rights.

Equality of opportunity All people should start with the same possibility of succeeding and developing.

Foundational equality People are born equal and therefore entitled to equal protection of the law.

Formal equality Equality of opportunity is protected through formal laws.

Meritocracy Social, economic and political advancement should be based on individual worth and ability.

■ **Social liberalism:** actively promoting toleration by passing laws to punish those who are not tolerant of others.

Key thinkers include:
■ Thomas Hill Green
■ John Rawls
■ Betty Friedan

Debates within liberalism

Classical and modern liberalism disagree over:
■ negative and positive freedoms
■ the size and role of the state
■ rates of taxation
■ laissez-faire and Keynesian capitalism
■ levels of democracy and respect for private property

Classical and modern liberalism agree over:
■ a positive view of human nature
■ the importance of individualism
■ rationalism and toleration
■ the principle of capitalism
■ a government based on consent and limited by constitutional protections

> ### Key terms
>
> **Laissez-faire capitalism**
> The economy should be left to market forces, without interference from the government such as duties, tariffs, taxes and regulations.
>
> **Keynesian capitalism**
> The government should intervene in the economy, spending money to maintain full employment.

Key thinkers

Table 100 **Key thinkers and themes**

Thinker	Human nature	State	Society	Economy
John Locke	Humans are rational and self-interested, but mindful of others	Rules by the consent of the governed (the social contract). The state only has fiduciary power	Natural rights guide social relations, not laws	The state should respect private property and act as a neutral arbiter
Mary Wollstonecraft	Men and women are rational beings, yet women lacked equality	Republican but wanted women's rights enshrined in the constitution. Defended the French Revolution arguing people had a right to rebel against a government that did not protect them	A patriarchal and aristocratic society undermined female individualism	Liberated women would boost a free-trade economy
John Stuart Mill	Human nature is progressing to higher levels than simple hedonism. Liberty enables individualism	Representative democracy with respect for minority rights. The law can restrict other-regarding actions if they are potentially harmful, but not self-regarding actions	A society of individuality and self-improvement. Society should be based on utilitarianism — actions that lead to general happiness should be favoured	Laissez-faire capitalism was the route to a happy and successful society

►

Thinker	Human nature	State	Society	Economy
Thomas Hill Green	Positive freedom allows humans self-development to contribute to the greater good	State should help the poor to have positive freedom, not simply negative freedom	The poor need education, better housing, better working conditions, better food	Capitalism needs to be moderated, otherwise hereditary privilege and poverty will prevent positive freedom
John Rawls	All humans are selfish and empathetic. They all deserve equal rights	The state has a duty to assist the less fortunate	The condition of the poorest should be improved	Free-market capitalism should be restricted on the basis of distributive justice
Betty Friedan	Human nature, marriage and motherhood discourages self-advancement for women	The state has a duty to prevent discrimination against women and ensure equal rights	Society is chauvinistic with women being complicit in this. Civil rights and feminist movements were needed in the USA	Anti-discrimination legislation would boost the free market

Key terms

Fiduciary power The state only has authority as long as it acts in the best interests of its people.

Hedonism Pleasure-seeking as the ultimate aim.

Individualism Freedom allows individuals to pursue their unique talents and goals.

Other-regarding actions Actions that affect others.

Self-regarding actions Actions that only affect one's self.

Utilitarianism Ethical theory based on happiness: actions that increase the happiness (utility) of the majority of the population are good, actions that make people unhappy are bad.

Distributive justice Society should allow maximum freedom for individuals, provided that this does not restrict others' liberty. Inequalities should only be allowed if the poorest benefit more than they would if resources were allocated more equally.

Synoptic link

Betty Friedan was the co-founder and first president of US pressure group the National Organisation for Women (NOW). She helped to launch the second wave of American feminism.

Do you know?

1 What are the core ideas and principles of liberalism?
2 How do the core ideas and principles relate to human nature, the state, society and the economy?
3 What different types of liberalism exist?
4 On which areas do the different types agree and disagree?
5 Which types of liberalism are the core thinkers associated with?

4.2 Conservatism

You need to know
- the core ideas of conservatism
- the differing views and tensions within conservatism
- the key ideas of:
  - ☐ Hobbes
  - ☐ Burke
  - ☐ Oakeshott
  - ☐ Rand
  - ☐ Nozick
- how these thinkers' ideas relate to human nature, the state, society and the economy

Conservatism was an ideological reaction against liberalism:
- Conservative thinkers were shocked by the violence and chaos of the French Revolution.
- They promoted a return to social hierarchy and order with limited change when needed.
- Deference to superiors, respect for traditional institutions and a negative view of human behaviour underpinned their thinking.

Core ideas

Table 101 **Core ideas of conservatism**

Idea	Meaning	Related concepts
Pragmatism	▪ Decisions are made based on what is needed and beneficial, rather than ideology	Organic society
Tradition	▪ Traditional customs and methods provide structure to society ▪ Lessons should be drawn from history and experience ▪ Change should happen slowly and in small steps	Respect for private property Nation-state Empiricism Christian democracy
Human imperfection	▪ Behaviour is shaped by environment, not by individuals ▪ Humans are inherently selfish and need to be controlled through laws and restrictions	Original sin Judaeo-Christian morality Order and authority
Organic society	▪ Society is more important than the individual. Individual freedoms may need to be limited for the good of society ▪ Society emerges over time and evolves without being created	Tradition
Paternalism	▪ Society works best when it is unequal ▪ The wisest, strongest and wealthiest should govern society and take responsibility for the lower classes	Hierarchy Noblesse oblige A ruling class

Idea	Meaning	Related concepts
Libertarianism	■ Supports free markets and individual liberty within a nation state ■ Individual freedoms should be respected by governments	Laissez-faire Thatcherism Neo-liberalism

Key terms

Empiricism Judgements based on experience. This leads to pragmatic rather than ideological decision making.

Human imperfection Humanity is inherently flawed so perfection is unattainable.

Authority A higher degree of power or status over others. Conservatives feel that the ruling elite's authority is justified as they believe it results in good government.

Hierarchy The idea that there will naturally be a system of social or class structures with superior and inferior members.

Noblesse oblige The paternalistic duty of those in power.

Free market An economic system in which the government does not interfere with the forces of supply and demand.

Types of conservatism

Traditional conservatism

Traditional conservatism believes in:
■ human imperfection
■ authority is needed to control society through a social hierarchy, but those in control hold *noblesse oblige*
■ society and reforms should be based on experience and tradition, and limited
■ society is organic and needs to change to conserve the best of the past
■ class divisions are inevitable
■ a society of little communities

Key term

Change to conserve Limited amounts of change are necessary to prevent more radical revolutions.

Key thinkers include:
■ Thomas Hobbes
■ Edmund Burke

One-nation conservatism

One-nation conservatism believes in:
■ a society of classes within a strong nation state
■ paternalistic duty of the rich to look after the poor
■ state-sponsored social reform to counteract the permissive society
■ restrictions on laissez-faire capitalism

- support for Keynesian economics, welfare states and mixed economies
- pragmatic approaches

Key thinkers include:
- Michael Oakeshott

New-right conservatism

New-right conservatism believes in:
- individual freedom and atomism
- reduction in taxation and government spending
- reducing the size of the state
- laissez-faire capitalism and free markets with deregulation and privatisation
- private property
- minimal government and reduction of welfare
- tougher law and order
- strong national defence
- restrictions on immigration
- traditional social values and anti-permissiveness

Key thinkers include:
- Ayn Rand
- Robert Nozick

The new right is also fragmented into:
- **Neo-liberalism:** focused on individualism and free-market economics.
- **New-conservatism:** focused on tradition and the maintenance of traditional social and cultural values through law and order.

Comparing types of conservatism

Traditional, one-nation and new-right conservatism disagree over:
- a sceptical or positive view of human nature
- society: one of small communities or one that is the sum of individuals
- a strong and powerful nation state or a small and minimalist state
- the extent of free-market capitalism

Traditional, one-nation and new-right conservatism agree over:
- humanity being motivated by self-interest
- government exists to provide national security and maintain law and order
- the importance of law and order
- society is fractured
- respect for private property
- the principle of free-market capitalism

> ### Key term
>
> **Atomism** Society is composed of self-interested and self-serving individuals.
>
> **Anti-permissiveness** A rejection of the cultural reforms of the 1960s and 1970s.

> ### Synoptic link
>
> British prime minister Margaret Thatcher (1979–90) and US president Ronald Reagan (1981–89) were both part of the New Right.

> ### Exam tip
>
> Remember that new-right conservatism is more ideological than earlier, more pragmatic, forms of conservatism. Rather than conserving existing structures, it aims to dramatically reduce the size of the state and allow unrestricted free markets.

Key thinkers

Table 102 **Key thinkers and themes**

Thinker	Human nature	State	Society	Economy
Thomas Hobbes	Individuals are selfish and ruthless. Without government a primitive 'state of nature' would exist, which would be 'nasty, brutish and short'	Government exists to provide security and order. Peace is the first 'natural law' and humans must submit to the authority of the sovereign in order to allow natural law to rule	Society emerges from the social contract between individuals to leave the state of nature and submit to the authority of the sovereign for self-protection	The economy can only exist through the authority of the sovereign
Edmund Burke	Humans desire, but cannot achieve, perfection	The state is organic and aristocratic. As a member of the Whig party, Burke believed government should not have absolute power. Supported American Revolution as it conserved the ancient right of the people to 'no taxation without representation'. Condemned the Jacobins of the French Revolution as a destructive break with past tradition	Society is based on small communities ('little platoons'). Did not believe in the social contract, instead society developed organically over time, passing down important traditions and institutions	Free markets and laissez-faire
Michael Oakeshott	Humanity should be free within structures. Humans do best when supported by traditions based on years of experience. Rationalism is dangerous as it replaces sound traditions with abstract ideas that will fail	Government by tradition and pragmatism. Argued for 'politics of scepticism' rather than 'politics of faith'	Humanity depends on local communities	Free markets need to be moderated
Ayn Rand	Humans should by guided by rational and ethical egoism (self-interest and self-fulfilment). It is morally right to prioritise one's individual rights and happiness above everything	Minimal role (law, order and security). Opposed collectivism and statism	There is no society, only a mass of individuals (atomism)	Free markets with no state intervention
Robert Nozick	Individuals have self-ownership so human liberty is essential	The state passes public works to private sectors. State has very limited functions	Society should promote individual self-fulfilment	The state should only be an arbiter between private companies. Inequalities of wealth resulting from freely exchanged contracts are fair, whereas any redistribution of wealth is an attack on freedom

Key terms

Rationalism Basing society on abstract reasoning and political philosophy.

Politics of scepticism Assumes that the government is unable to fix humanity's problems, so should play a limited role.

Politics of faith Assumes that the government can improve conditions for humanity, perhaps creating a perfect world.

Collectivism A system in which the individual is seen as less important than the collective group.

Statism A system in which the state controls most of society and the economy.

Do you know?

1 What are the core principles of conservatism?
2 What are typical conservative attitudes to human nature, the state, society and the economy?
3 What are the tensions within conservative ideology?
4 What are the areas where the different types agree and disagree?
5 Which types of conservatism are the core thinkers associated with?

4.3 Socialism

You need to know

- the core ideas of socialism
- the differing views and tensions within socialism
- the key ideas of:
  - ☐ Marx and Engels
  - ☐ Luxemburg
  - ☐ Webb
  - ☐ Crosland
  - ☐ Giddens
- how these thinkers' ideas relate to human nature, the state, society and the economy

Socialism emerged over the nineteenth century:

- It was a reaction to traditional conservatism and the inequality that had emerged in capitalist industrial societies.
- It promoted the idea of collective action and the removal of all hierarchy.
- It promised a system that would ensure economic equality for all.

Core ideas

Table 103 **Core ideas of socialism**

Idea	Meaning	Related concepts
Collectivism	<ul><li>Human society will be strongest when there is collective action by all humanity towards a greater good</li><li>Politics, economics and social reform should benefit society, not individuals</li><li>There should be wealth redistribution to equalise society</li></ul>	Common ownership Progressive taxation Progressive public spending Public services
Common humanity	<ul><li>Humans are naturally social</li><li>Individuals are shaped by society and capitalism has corrupted natural social tendencies</li></ul>	Anti-capitalism Fraternity
Equality	<ul><li>Belief that people are not born equal.</li><li>Focus on equality of outcome, rather than of opportunity</li></ul>	Social justice
Social class	<ul><li>Capitalist society is divided into classes. The class that owns the means of production (bourgeoisie) benefits at the expense of the working class (proletariat)</li><li>Class analysis argues that capitalism is based on the exploitation of the working class</li></ul>	Class consciousness
Workers' control	<ul><li>Those who produce should control the means of production</li><li>A strong state is necessary to achieve a socialist state, but that state should be governed by the workers</li></ul>	Communism Marxism

Key terms

Common ownership The means of production are owned collectively and profits are shared.

Fraternity The relationship between people.

Capitalism Wealth is privately owned and economies are driven by market forces.

Social justice An attempt to limit inequality through wealth redistribution.

Equality of outcome Aiding disadvantaged groups to achieve the same outcomes as other groups.

Class consciousness A self-understanding of a class by its members.

Communism All wealth and society are organised and shared communally.

Marxism The political theories of Karl Marx that communism is inevitable.

Types of socialism

Revolutionary socialism

Revolutionary socialism believes in:

- the destruction of the capitalist system
- the overthrow of the existing world order
- the 'creation' of a socialist state
- total state control over the economy
- a socialist or communist state would be governed by a dictatorship of the proletariat
- imposition of socialism on society
- common ownership

Key thinkers include:

- Karl Marx and Friedrich Engels
- Rosa Luxemburg

Exam tip

Be careful not to confuse 'revolutionary' with 'evolutionary'; 'evolutionary' means gradual change, while 'revolutionary' means rapid change. Both types of socialism agree on change but disagree on the speed of change.

Democratic socialism

Democratic socialism believes in:

- the replacement of the capitalist system by a socialist system
- that a socialist state can evolve from current systems without revolution
- a socialist state will be achieved by socialist parties winning electoral majorities
- nationalisation and common ownership

Key thinkers include:

- Beatrice Webb

Social democracy

Social democracy is a branch of revisionist socialism, that believes capitalism and socialism can be compatible, unlike fundamental socialism, which believes capitalism must be eradicated to create a socialist state.

Social democrats believe in:

- rationality
- evolutionary socialism
- operating within current political structures
- a mixed economy, with socialistic elements operating within a capitalist framework
- major state involvement in the economy

Key terms

Revisionist socialism
An approach to socialism that believes socialism is compatible with capitalism.

Evolutionary socialism
Socialism will gradually be achieved within existing systems.

- nationalisation of some private industry
- Keynesian economics
- persuading voters of the inevitable benefits of socialism through social justice

Key thinkers include:
- Anthony Crosland

Third way

Third way believes in:
- a greater focus on equality of opportunity rather than equality of outcome
- liberalisation of the economy to provide more money for public spending
- privatisation over nationalisation
- a greater focus on social and political equality as well as economic equality

Key thinkers include:
- Anthony Giddens

Comparing types of socialism

Revolutionary, democratic socialism, social democrats and third-way supporters disagree over:
- the impact of society on human nature
- how far human nature is corrupted by capitalism
- the strength and power of the state
- the speed and nature of change
- the existence or role of capitalism within a socialist state

Revolutionary, democratic socialism, social democrats and third-way supporters agree that:
- human nature is social and malleable
- a nation state is essential
- change and reforms are needed to the current system
- the state has a duty to oversee public welfare
- the state plays a part in the economic developments

> **Synoptic link**
>
> Tony Blair's adoption of the third way was crucial to his 1997 landslide victory.

Key thinkers

Table 104 **Key thinkers and themes**

Thinker	Human nature	State	Society	Economy
Karl Marx and Friedrich Engels	Humans are social creatures, but this has been damaged by capitalism. Marx and Engels developed the theory of dialectical materialism.	Existing governments will be inevitably destroyed by revolution and replaced by a socialist state. A dictatorship of the proletariat will create a classless society. The state will become unnecessary	Society should be classless. All history has been 'the history of class struggles'. Society will eventually replace the state taking 'from each according to his ability, to each according to his needs'	Abolition of private property and collective ownership of means of production
Rosa Luxemburg	Social cohesion exists within social classes	Existing governments will be destroyed and replaced by a workers-based society. Tight party organisation of workers is not required as structure will emerge later	Class consciousness and material conditions will result in an inevitable spontaneous mass strike by workers	The mass strike will overthrow capitalism and replace it with an economy based on workers' control
Beatrice Webb	Capitalism should be replaced by an evolutionary process	Universal suffrage would inevitably lead to the working class voting for a socialist state	Poverty must be tackled	Gradual replacement of capitalism by common ownership of the means of production. Webb investigated and supported the cooperative movement, particularly cooperative federalism
Anthony Crosland	Humans naturally oppose inequality. Importance of personal liberty	Existing systems can be used to create a socialist state	Social democracy would reduce social inequality through the welfare state and comprehensive education	A mixed economy. As a revisionist Crosland criticised Marx and argued that nationalisation need not be the primary goal of socialists
Anthony Giddens	Social fairness is combined with self-fulfilment	Government power should be decentralised	Socialists must work with the middle classes, not oppose them	A neo-liberal economy to provide for welfare programmes

Key term

Dialectical materialism The philosophy that the human mind or spirit, and its ideas, are determined by the material context in which they exist. They cannot exist independently of material circumstances. This leads to historical materialism, in which history is determined by the struggle between different groups that results from material differences, e.g. bourgeoisie and proletariat in a capitalist society.

Key terms

Cooperative movement Movement of collective ownership of cooperative organisations. Webb developed the idea of cooperative individualism, in which workers form collectively owned organisations, and cooperative federalism, in which consumers own the businesses that they buy from.

Revisionist Someone who contradicts the established ideas of previous thinkers.

Do you know?

1 What are the main ideas upon which socialism rests?
2 How does socialism relate to human nature, the state, society and the economy?
3 What are the different types of socialism?
4 What are the areas of agreement and disagreement within socialism?
5 Which types of socialism are the core thinkers associated with?

End of section 4 questions

1 What are the core ideas of liberalism?
2 How do the core ideas of liberalism relate to human nature, society, the state and the economy?
3 Why is there tension between the different strands of liberalism?
4 What are the common traits of liberalism?
5 How do different thinkers relate to different strands of liberalism?
6 What are the core ideas of conservatism?
7 How do the core ideas of conservatism relate to human nature, society, the state and the economy?
8 Why is there tension between the different strands of conservatism?
9 How do different thinkers relate to different strands of conservatism?
10 What are the common traits of conservatism?
11 What are the core ideas of socialism?
12 How do the core ideas of socialism relate to human nature, society, the state and the economy?
13 Why is there tension between the different strands of socialism?
14 How do different thinkers relate to different strands of socialism?
15 What are the common traits of socialism?